Fit-For-Purpose
Leadership #3

LeadershipGigs

WRITING MATTERS PUBLISHING

Fit-For-Purpose Leadership #3

First published in April 2018

Writing Matters Publishing (UK)
info@writingmatterspublishing.com
www.writingmatterspublishing.com

ISBN 978-1-9999187-7-4

Editor: Andrew Priestley

Contributors:
Health: Nick Powell, Menno Siebinga
Meaning and Purpose: Fran Boorman, Susan Bryant
Mindset: Naeem Arif, Dr Kylie Hutchings Mangion, Ches Moulton, Tony Jeton Selimi
Social/Relationships: Matthew Newnham
Best Practice: Lucy Barkas, Diana Barnett, Simon Hammond, Andrew Priestley
Emerging Trends: Robyn Wilson, Michele Scataglini

Dedication

Dedicated to business leaders everywhere
- and to you - someone who has decided to
positively change *your* world.

Contents

About Leadership Gigs

Leadership Gigs was launched in January 2017 as a global, invitation-only, *WhatsApp* community, for business leaders - CEOs, MDs, executives, business owners and entrepreneurs.

This unique community was created in response to the need of leaders for candid, authentic, conversations with like-minded peers. Most leaders don't feel they can have that level of openness with work colleagues.

Leadership Gigs works because it allows them to have totally confidential discussions with their peers with a broad base of experience and from a diverse range of industries.

The glue, of course, is *Trust.*

Leadership Gigs offers a safe forum for bouncing ideas off one another, sharing, discussing, reflecting and receiving candid, constructive feedback. But importantly it allows them to de-role, share concerns, doubts, express vulnerability and get honest and direct support.

Feedback suggests that being able to talk freely with other business leaders reduces stress and isolation and leads to insights, key light bulb moments and breakthroughs.

The calibre of leaders and the candid exchange in *Leadership Gigs* is practical, insightful, inspiring but above all open and honest.

Welcome to Fit For Purpose Leadership 3

This is *Leadership Gigs'* third *Fit For Purpose Leadership* outing. *Leadership Gigs* is a growing global think tank of business leaders committed to developing highly effective business leaders.

The big leadership issues we identified for books 1 and 2 still seem to be relevant: *Health, Mindset, Meaning and Purpose, Social/Relationships, Best Practice* and *Emerging Trends.*

Machine or Value Environment?

According to Ralph D Stacey (2009) an emerging trend is rethinking the long standing view that an organisation is a myopic, insular, machine model where workers are lower part of a hierarchy effectively lead by a leader/manager who is authoritative, strong, decisive and singularly omniscient.

In this model the leader is an engineer/puppeteer controlling, directing and manipulating mechanistic elements and the human resources are directed to do what they are told to do to deliver value.

The global financial crisis that kicked off in 2009 irrevocably changed our perspective of the all-knowing, infallible leader.

We are only just emerging from a massive socio-economic downturn which demonstrated that many so-called business leaders were far from infallible or immune from business failure. This has lead many organisations to rethink their organisational models.

And leadership.

What we are seeing now are emerging models of leadership that focus on co-leading - more than one CEO - with a greater emphasis on creativity, relationships and importantly the recognition that organisations are more interdependent, complex human adaptive systems rather than simple, linear mechanistic systems.

We are starting to seeing fast growth, peak performance organisations transitioning from a focus on the individual (part) to the collective (whole). Notably, the best ones have been building adaptive systems for over a decade. They had to.

The best leaders are moving from controlling individuals to do what they are told, to creating conditions in the environment that your people adapt and self-regulate, that deliver value.

But what does that mean to you?

Organisational change aside, it still infers that the leader develops skills and knowledge that enable them to facilitate or co-create a dynamic, best-practice adaptive environment.

Leaders are not infallible, all-wise or all-knowing and Stacey's research raises important leadership development issues for modern day leaders. Importantly, Stacey clearly makes the case for balancing wellbeing and wellness, relationships and inclusive dialogue within the context of commercial reality.

After all we are *business* leaders first and foremost.

With that clearly in mind, *Fit For Purpose Leadership #3* explores some of the best thinking around enhancing your personal and professional abilities as a leader in any sized business and any leadership context.

We diligently revisited our categories and our subject headers and agreed that they are still relevant.

- **Health:** Nick Powell and Menno Siebinga explore issues directly related to health and leadership.
- **Meaning and Purpose:** Fran Boorman and Susan Bryant explore factors linked to long-term role satisfaction and legacy.
- **Mindset:** Naeem Arif, Dr Kylie Hutchings Mangion, Ches Moulton and Tony Jeton Selimi provide four articulate and unique takes on your mental game.
- **Relationships:** Matthew Newnham delivers a thought provoking article on energy and conversations that flow.
- **Best Practice:** Lucy Barkas, Diana Barnett, Simon Hammond and Andrew Priestley give four perspectives on *'what does good look like?'*
- **Emerging Trends:** Robyn Wilson and Michele Scataglini explore new directions in business leadership as it relates to neuroscience, disruption and technology.

Again, welcome and enjoy. Of course, if you would like to know more about joining the conversation in *Leadership Gigs,* please go to <insert page>

Reference

- Stacey, R.D. (2009). *Complexity and Organisational Reality.* Routledge.

Health

Physical health, fitness, exercise, wellness, wellbeing, nutrition, diet, exercise, nutrition, sleep, hydration, hormones, genetics, DNA

Putting Yourself First as a Leader

Nick Powell

When I work with my clients I often ask them to think about how they should be prioritising their lives from the perspective of work, health and family. Friends could fall into the family category and community interests could fall into the work category.

In the majority of cases the answer is:

Family, health then work

When I ask them how they are actually prioritising their lives, the answer is:

Work, family and then health

I believe that neither answer is correct. If you truly want to have wonderful relationships at home and put yourself in the best position to take your business and career to new heights, you need to become selfish and put yourself first.

Many Clients shudder when I ask them to be selfish, so I always follow up with 'what's wrong in putting yourself first in the service of others?' It's a similar concept to what we all hear in the safety briefings on planes prior to take off: "when the oxygen mask drops down, please attach your own mask before helping others"

Meet John ...

John was chronically stressed from work and was putting all of his efforts into reaching his next leadership position. As a direct result of the stress, he was self-medicating with alcohol, cutting back on sleep, not spending quality time with his fiancée and reaching a stage of chronic burnout. John wasn't making the right decisions, his work was suffering and so was his relationship, which sadly ended.

John decided to focus on himself and build a handful of habits that would serve him well, help manage stress and set up every day for success.

Within four months John transformed his life to the point where he had got married to the love of his life, he was expecting his first child and doubled his salary by moving to a new role at a new Company.

There is real power in putting yourself first and amazing things start to happen when you do so and the world around you will slot into place.

When you put yourself first, you aren't only focusing on your physical health but also your emotional and mental health. You need to look holistically at what is going on in your life and ensure you set yourself up for success and by putting yourself first you're in the best place to serve others as a leader, a parent, a spouse and a friend.

A state of health is binary for many people; you're sick or you're not, you have a condition, or you don't but in reality, it's much more nuanced and there is a sliding scale between supreme health and disease.

The secret to maintaining your health is to manage your mitochondria. I'll avoid giving you a deep Science lesson but from your school days you may recall that mitochondria are the tiny organelles that live in every cell in your body and are responsible for all energy production in your body and telling your individual cells to live or die.

Your mitochondria is important to your health, energy and overall wellbeing. Look after them and you'll live a long, happy and energised life.

If you are suffering with low energy levels, then it's likely that your mitochondria aren't functioning as well as they should be which increases your risk of serious health conditions. I always ask my clients to rate their current energy levels compared to when they were in their early twenties. How are your energy levels compared to an earlier time in your life?

Let me tell you above Dave.

Dave was 38 and working successfully as an independent management consultant, working with a number of global organisations delivering change programmes. He had built a great reputation and was always in demand for work.

The problem, was that Dave was overweight, suffering with low energy levels and was starting to struggle to focus in the afternoons and at the end of the week.

He wasn't ill but didn't feel well and the zing and sparkle was disappearing out of life and he felt like he wasn't achieving his full potential.

Dave worked hard during the week and then used the weekend to recover and wasn't fully present with his family. He thought this was normal and just a part of coming up to 40.

I am Dave and I was wrong … there is no reason why you can't feel as great when you're 40 or 60 as you did when you were 20. You need to prioritise yourself, your energy levels and your health.

If you are unsure if you are suffering from mitochondria energy issues, here are a few things for you to look out for:

- Inability to focus; allowing yourself to procrastinate and get distracted
- Stress, tiredness and running on adrenaline
- Negative mood
- Poor motivation
- Using will power to get things done
- Brain fog – you have x10 more mitochondria in your brain

If you suffer from any of the above, you aren't putting yourself first, it's impacting your performance today and it's likely to impact your long-term health.

Taking action
Here are five foundational actions that I use with my clients that deliver extraordinary results:

Prime your day for success
Setting your day up for success is such a simple yet powerful action that will enable you to set your intentions for the day and enable you to achieve the things that puts you in the best possible place physically, mentally and emotionally.

You can prime your day for success through a morning ritual where you string a series of good habits together and perform the same ritual each and every day until it becomes habitual like taking a shower or cleaning your teeth.

I recommend you include the following in your morning ritual:

- Drink at least 500ml of water
- Take supplements based on your specific needs
- Move / exercise (high intensity interval training, stretching, yoga)
- Meditate
- Journal and express gratitude
- Ensure you take care of the usual hygiene
- Eat a healthy and low carbohydrate breakfast

Things *not to do* as part of your morning ritual are:

- Checking email and social media – keep your phone on aeroplane mode until you are ready to start work
- Planning out your day (this should be done the day before)
- Completing tasks

Help tame your monkey mind with mindfulness

Having a daily meditation practice has had a massive impact on my own personal performance over the past year. I was of the opinion that it was all a bit *woo woo* and not for me but having understood the Science and experienced the benefits, I'm sold. In his book *Tools of Titans*, Tim Ferriss interviewed the world's top performers in their fields and 80% of the people he interviewed have a mindfulness practice.

Mindfulness has helped tame a very strong inner critic that would constantly push me to do better at the expense of my health and my relationships. I can honestly say that my day always goes better if I've taken the time to meditate that morning.

There are many different forms of meditation, the easiest way to experience it is to download an App onto your phone. Popular ones are *Headspace, Calm* and *10% Happier*.

High intensity interval training (HIIT)

Managing your time and fitting everything into a busy life is a continual struggle that we all can relate to but unfortunately, exercise often comes at the bottom of the list.

If you're not currently exercising, don't know where to start and are struggling for time then check out the 7-minute work-out. There are plenty of apps, *YouTube* videos and instructions online and all you need is a chair, a timer and yourself. Start off with the 7-minute workout and as you get more comfortable, repeat it twice (14 mins) and then three times (21 mins). 21 minutes two/three times a week is all you need to get outstanding results.

If you really enjoy the gym and find it a great outlet for stress then try incorporating HIIT into your workout, whether it's cardio or strength training work. I have found that many people spend hours in the gym each week and the same results could be achieved in a fraction of the time, giving them much needed time back.

Eat what makes you feel great

Discussing nutrition has become as taboo as sex, politics and religion around the dinner party table and with so many different types of diet - vegetarian, vegan, low carb, ketogenic, 5:2 etc, there is so much debate on what works and what doesn't.

The truth is, what works for you, probably doesn't work for me because our bodies are different. We will both metabolise macro-nutrients differently, are sensitive to different foods and our gut microbiome responds better to some foods than others.

Eat what makes you feel great. If you don't feel great and highly energised after a meal, there was something in your last meal that you shouldn't have eaten.

If you have eaten something your body doesn't like then you are likely to experience bloating in the stomach, brain fog and fatigue.

Try removing the following from your diet for 30 days and see how you feel afterwards: all refined sugars, grains, dairy, vegetable oils, potatoes and processed foods. For the 30 days, listen to your body after each meal and see what else may be causing you problems.

Improve the quality, not quantity of your sleep

So how many hours do people think is the optimal amount to sleep at night? It's a personal choice; I've slept on average seven hours per night for the past 12 months.

However, focus on quality and not quantity – start by downloading the *Sleep Cycle* app, which will monitor your quality and duration of sleep. You will start to notice correlations between what you have done that day and how well you sleep.

A few tips to improving sleep quality:

- Sleep in a dark 'cave' – block all LED lights in your bedroom
- Avoid blue light – install f.lux on your PC/ Mac and dim the lights 2 hours before bedtime.
- If you can, wear blue blocking glasses 1 hour before bed.
- Don't drink caffeine after 2pm
- Supplement with magnesium before bed
- Write a journal before bed to get thoughts out of your head
- Add a spoonful of honey and apple cider vinegar to decaffeinated tea and drink it 20 mins before bed

This is just a short selection of practices that will add almost immediate benefits. The key to success with any of the above suggestions, of course, is consistency.

About Nick Powell

Nick is the founder of *Stronger Self*, a peak performance coach, business consultant and charity trustee. He works with high achieving entrepreneurs and senior leaders to enable them to put themselves first and take their personal and business performance to the next level.

Nick's approach has been scientifically proven using the best of breed cutting edge tools and techniques from the worlds of productivity, anti-aging, biohacking and neuroscience, harnessing the exciting intersection between biology and technology.

Nick is a certified coach by one of the world's leading human performance organisations, Bulletproof 360 and has spent hundreds of hours discovering the secrets of the world's top performers to understand how they hack their own biology to release massive amounts of untapped energy, enabling them to take their personal and business performance to the next level.

www.strongerself.co.uk

https://www.linkedin.com/in/nickpowell/

Don't Stop Ahead Of Your Time

Menno Siebinga

"More people die every year because they stop with living than dying itself."

Menno Siebinga

Be warned, this is not a story with a happy ending, but it could postpone your ending. This is a story about how can you maintain and thrive. So you don't need to experience a part of your life has to stop with living before you die.

I was about seven when my dad was 59 and stopped working, or I better say *he had to stop working*. He was a doctor, one of the good old ones his old clients used to say. He did by himself what 2-½ doctors are doing now.

For seven years he took care of his seven children from his first marriage by himself. He co-founded a company on the side, which currently 45 years later employs more than 300 people. At 50, he found new love in my mom and became a father again at age 52.

My dad's work was his passion and life, yet he had to quit. He couldn't continue anymore; he was utterly exhausted and drained. In the years to come, it would get worse, even to the point that my mom asked all his kids to visit because they thought he would die soon.

He recovered, but he never worked again.

He continued to dream for decades on a regular basis about his work.

In our western society, it is normal for most people that the day you start a working life, you should also start building up a financial pension.

But almost everyone also forgets to start building up a body and brain pension. Because you can have all the money in the world, but it won't matter that much if you don't have enough body and brain capacity to enjoy it.

I think its very important that leaders lead by example as well as give their staff the tools to start building enough body and brain capital on their figurative bank account, so they have enough for now and later, for work, home and retirement.

One of the body and brain accounts you have is your daily energy account.

The problem with my dad and most high performers are that they are very crafted in how they spend this account but are often terrible at making sure they put enough back for the next day.

When we look at why my dad had to stop working, it wasn't an overnight thing. It was a process of many years continuing to work while not fully recovering. I often compared it to an accident, but then one, which takes places over weeks or years. The difference with this one is that it is an accumulation of many small accidents, from which they don't fully or not at all recover, and this starts building up.

In top sports, 1% more improvement makes a huge difference. 1% more and better recovery can do the same. Less recovery can't just affect your productivity, but can also make you more accident-prone. Doing more then you know you should do, is possible. It's just not sustainable plus it usually goes hand in hand with lending energy from tomorrow.

So why it is that we often don't fully recover?

One thing is around the way we think about energy. Our energy works pretty similarly like a car. Most people have the juvenile thinking that at any moment in the day they should have 100% energy. And they do, only not in the way most people think.

When a car has a full tank, it can drive far, and it has 100% of the energy. When it is half full, it can go a lot less further, but still has 100%. Because it has 100% of the energy it has at that given moment, and that's what you have to work with. If you have 5 litres in your car, you wouldn't' try to drive a distance which would take 10 litres, and be pissed at the car for not getting you there. When it comes down to ourselves, we will get pissed at ourselves for not getting to where we want.

Just remember you always have a 100% energy level at any given moment. That 100% just goes up and down the whole time and that is what you have to work with.

Another thinking mistake leaders and staff make comes down to the question that I often ask people. Which one is stronger your body or your brain? Almost everyone says your brain. To me, your brain is not stronger. It is more important. If you chose to always ask more of your body then it can, your body will eventually stop working along. And no matter how badly your brain wants it, your body is not able to co-operate any more. It is like a relationship where the secret is to give and take and work together.

Another mistake we see is that people don't take action. When we see an accident, we all recognise it, and we would right away react to it and see how we can help. The amazing thing is that with the small accidents in ourselves, we also would recognise them most of the time. We just don't act upon them. Thinking time will heal them; it will go away by itself. It's like the standardised SOS sign. If you don't react to it, the sign will get louder to get your attention, and eventually, it could be too late, more damage, more accident prone or at a point of no return.

Imagine holding a toothbrush on the level of your teeth. This is quite easy, but imagine you need to keep it there for a day, or a week. Despite the small weight, it will get you because there is no recovery. If you need to hold up a toothbrush for one day and can take short breaks every time, it suddenly becomes very doable.

This both works for your body and brain.

One simple way I use with my clients to recover more fully, and doesn't need technology, cognitive testing, smartphones, health checks, is done with a piece of paper and pen. You ask yourself these questions preferably at the same moment every day and draw it on the scale (you can download this file for free and print it on *superagers.eu/daily-check*

1. Today on the moments I was active how much energy did I use? Draw the lines going up.
2. Was this more then I could/ had? Or was it just enough or did I have more?
3. On the moments that I wasn't active how much did I recover/recharge/discharge?

With these three questions, you can see I was or wasn't fully recovered when you went back to work.

If you did recover fully, congratulations, you are one of the few.

If you didn't fully recover, ask yourself where you can make small adjustments. Was it the load or the duration? To help with this you can download a file for free on:

www.superagers.eu/daily-check-actionsheet

This is one of the best and easiest ways to keep track of your daily energy for body and brain account and keep a positive balance. Remember it's a lot easier to keep what you have, then to lose it and have to regain it back.

I hope that soon everyone knows how to take care of their body and brain on a daily basis like we brush our teeth on a daily basis.

Vitality and healthy ageing are just like brushing your teeth.

Two extra points to why I think it is crucial to recovering more fully.

- To recover fully, you have to switch off, which means letting go. Letting go is very hard for a lot of people. They often don't know that letting go is the gateway to Flow, the state where you perform and feel at your best.

- For those productivity addicts who feel guilty when taking breaks or think it is a waste of time. This might help. Think about your best ideas, did you get them when you were doing something else or when you were thinking hard about them? The most common answer was when you were busy with something else, this is our subconscious mind at work. Which is a lot more creative than our conscious mind. But it takes you to formulate to which problem you want to get a solution and then completely let go of it and do something else. So while you take a break, you can still put your subconscious to work, which could do a much better job then you could find yourself.

To summarise it is vital to *Start on Time* and *Be on Time*.

Start on time #1

Create a culture where it becomes standard the moment someone starts working at your company also to start building enough body and brain for now and later. When they start you equip them already with tools so they can work, for example, a laptop. This is an even better and sustainable tool and investment.

Be On Time #1

Recognize, listen and act on the SOS as quickly and thoroughly as possible. This also goes for the SOS you see from other people. Things we often don't see from ourselves, are apparent to others. Please care and do share, it could make all the difference, and there might not be another moment. Giving feedback is also a *Flow Trigger*. It will help if the business culture is one of trust, openness and vulnerability.

Be On Time #2

Both your body and brain should arrive at the same time.

This means to recharge them as well and much as thoroughly possible. For example when you get to work, and you noticed you hadn't recovered fully. Know that what you have at that moment is 100% of what you have. That's what you have to work with or choose first to recharge more.

Be On Time #3

Don't try to be ahead of time. The last time when I heard my dad's voice was on the phone. It was just before my work, and in my brain, I was already occupied with my work. I wasn't entirely there. Be there.

Be on Time #4

Do you best to be more fully in the now, this is where you make all your best memories and moments in life. This is the only moment you have been waiting for and can act on.

My dad had to, unfortunately, stop working ahead of time. When he was 89, he still biked 30 to 70 kilometres every day.

One month before he died, he wrote in his diary, that he had to be careful with crossing the road with his bike. He wrote he should stop when crossing and then pass carefully.

He recognized the SOS, but he didn't act on time.

On 28th of June 2017, he didn't stop but right away crossed the road and got hit by a truck. He went into a coma and died five days later. When trying to pass he might try to gain seconds, but in doing so, he lost everything. After his death, people told us, that they often saw him crossing the road dangerously, but never shared this with him or his children. He didn't share his concern with us. I believe he died unnecessarily ahead of his time...

Start on time to apply these principles, so you and your staff hopefully don't need to stop doing what you love ahead of time.

The right time is now. So you can continue to feel more alive now than ever before doing what you love.

Making sure you get to fully experience the gift the world has to give to you and the world can fully experience the gift you have to give.

About Menno Siebinga

Menno Siebinga is a physiotherapist, *Superagers Coach* and *Vitality Planner*.

He specialises in unlocking levels of vitality and meaning in Leaders and Entrepreneurs, between 50 and 67, that they didn't know they had in them.

As a physiotherapist and son (he took care of his mom when she became locked inside of her own body because of an neurological disease) he noticed the widespread lack of awareness under the over 50's, their children, doctors and society of what is possible after 50. This causes all kinds of problems from stop doing what you love, to not being able to play with your grandkids, to feeling superfluous.

He since transformed many into *Superagers*. He made a 91-year-old stroller free, an 88-year-old 4 cm taller and he helped a 58-year-old build enough body and brain pension and be in her best shape ever.

Menno's vision is that by 2025 it will be as familiar that people know what to do on a daily basis for their body and brain and do it, as it is with brushing their teeth.

So people no matter the age or circumstance know how to forget to grow old and don't need to unnecessary or prematurely have to stop with living.

Menno Siebinga

Body & Brain Knowledge Institute

The Netherlands

info@bodyenbrein.nl

www.superagers.eu

https://www.linkedin.com/in/menno-siebinga-7896042/

Meaning and Purpose

Spiritual, values, ethics, moral behaviours, legacy, generativity, rehearsing the future

Becoming an Attraction Business

Fran Boorman

The conversation ended abruptly and this lovely, kind man could not get away from me fast enough! I hadn't offended him, he was just protecting himself from *people like me*. This was a response I had become accustomed to in my business and one I knew I had to do something about. This is the story about how I changed the rules of selling and turned repulsion into attraction.

All businesses need to sell, yet selling has a bad reputation. Every day, people are bombarded with sales messages. In the intricately connected world that we live there is so much noise that it is hard to get your company's message across. Most sales techniques just add to that noise. But there is a better way. The most valuable lesson I learned as a leader was how to stop selling and start creating something that people wanted to be part of, both as customers and as part of our team.

For over a decade I have been involved in direct selling and endured the bad reputation of the *money grabbing* sales people who preceded me. I promoted products and services that were ethical, best in their market, and had genuine benefits to the customers. The traditional sales techniques being used were not working. They were not bad, they were just outdated. The world has changed and to be successful, so must we.

The rise of technology has changed the rules and it is not just about disruptive technology.

The way people think, behave and feel has changed beyond recognition. Today, people are more connected than they have ever been, yet they feel lonelier. They are addicted to *likes* and superficial friendships. Watching the edited (and apparently perfect!) version of their acquaintance's lives leaves most people feeling unfulfilled, and with a deep desire for real human connection.

Technology has also granted us the most intimate connection to the rest of the world, and all its problems. This is known as *Global Localisation* (or *Glocal* for short). This presents some exciting opportunities and distinct challenges. It is now easier than ever to do business with someone on the other side of the world, but that also means your business is competing with millions of others. All those other businesses are also shouting their sales messages. Your customers have a lot more choice, and even getting heard by them is a challenge.

This *Glocal* atmosphere has also led to another interesting trend in the way that people see the world.

On the screens in our hands we get to see all the world's problems in intimate detail, and not just in carefully edited news reports. We get to see content made by real people, just like us, who may be suffering terrible tragedies. They may be on the other side of the world but as we spectate from the devices in our hands we feel a strong connection to these strangers.

This has led to people feeling very different about the world and their place in it. It's a combination of frustration and a desire to be empowered to make a difference. It's a world where people don't feel safe, so they want to live for today - even though studies into death rates from tragedies show that the world is actually safer than it has been in a century.

In the business world this is leading to customers scrutinising the companies they associate with. Companies that are succeeding are the ones who don't just consider these trends to be society's problem.

They are the ones who take it upon themselves to participate and become part of the solution to the challenges we all face. Everything changed when I realised that the power of my business was not just to make money but to also make an impact on the world.

I first started looking at the people around me, my team. While they might have originally started working for our organisation to earn money, this was not what was keeping them with us. As a team, we had instinctively created a wonderful culture that felt like a family. It dawned on me that the reason people stayed working within our team wasn't because of the money, it was because of how they felt.

When I dug a little deeper I found that behind the day-to-day mask they presented, every one of them was a little bit lonely and unfulfilled.

Your instant reaction to the statement above about loneliness and unfulfillment might be that I needed a better recruitment strategy!

However, the brutal truth is that this is how most people feel. Connected, but lonely and frustrated because they are looking at a world they don't know how to participate in. I would even be brave enough to have put myself in that category. When I went to work it wasn't the money that truly motivated me, it was the sense of belonging and fulfilment that I got. I, like everyone else, want to be part of something greater than just myself.

Engagement comes when there is a balance between money, fulfilment and belonging.

It wasn't just my team that felt this way. Our customers and prospective customers also needed more than just a service or product in exchange for money. They too want to feel like they belong. And they want to belong to something that matters. Ultimately, they don't just want to buy from us, they wanted to feel connected.

The most powerful way to lead a business forward is to create an atmosphere where people feel like they belong and are making a difference.

When companies start using their business as a force for good they stop chasing customers and start attracting supporters.

Supporters come in the form of the most dedicated and committed employees, and the most loyal customers. If a company finds a cause that people can get passionate enough about, then their customers will not only be attracted to them, they will become the most focused sales message, retelling your story for you. Everyone loves a good story. To get heard you need a great story about what you are doing, why you are doing it and how others can be part of that.

Whatever your business is, you have the ability to use it as a tool to do good in the world. I am not talking about charity. Charity is the act of *giving* money. To be effective you need to align your business with a cause.

A cause is about taking action.

That action could be ensuring that the materials for your products are sourced responsibly and then making that supply chain part of your story. Making a real human connection with the people and the community that supply your goods. When a customer buys your product, or when one of your team sells your product they are making a positive impact in the world. They are helping some of those people who they see on their screens. They are now not just buying a product, they are buying into the dream of a better world. They are beginning to live part of that dream.

Do you have a service-based business? How could you use your service to have a positive impact on the world? Each time you get a customer in your home territory, could your staff gift some of their time? Perhaps to deliver those services to someone elsewhere in the world where that wisdom would have a big impact.

This will give you customers who feel like they are making a responsible purchasing decision, and staff who will learn vast amounts from delivering in two very different environments.

There are so many ways that you can use your business as a force for good but it has to come from a place of authenticity. This is not something you can 'green wash'. You must find something that you whole-heartedly believe in so that you can lead your company forward with passion and conviction.

By using my business as a force for good I was able to create a meaningful connection between myself, my team and our customers. Our customers started telling our story, and we started feeling motivated and committed to our business and what we stood for. The business went from strength to strength and is now one of the highest performing in its sector.

When I tell people about my business, no longer do they run away. Instead, they lean forward and want to learn more. We stand out because we make a difference. People want to feel part of what we are doing and, even though we don't do this for the money, it has directly impacted our profits and success.

Business being used as a force for good does not just have to be about social enterprises. This is for every business who want to be successful.

How can you make an impact on the world, the people around you and your profitability?

About Fran Boorman

Fran Boorman in an expert in helping small businesses become more purpose driven to unlock their full potential. She built a network marketing business to turnover in excess of £8.5 million around her two young children. Her business became one of the fastest growing in its sector and she went on to inspire over 1000 other people to start their own business, teaching her methods to empower them to achieve their own success. Fran is also bestselling author and a professional speaker.

In a noisy marketplace Fran's vision is to help all small businesses find their voice and story by engaging in a higher purpose. Fran is a big believer that business is the tool to right the world's wrongs.

Her vision is to see all small business owners fulfilling their potential by making a difference in the world. Fran is focused on increasing the success of organisations by using business as a force for good.

She demonstrates how to stand out from the crowd, build engagement and do good.

Fran produces a regular blog to share her insights and help businesses move forward.

Please connect with Fran on: *www.fran.global* and social media:

Facebook /Twitter/LinkedIn and Instagram: @FranBGlobal

Leadership In Families - Leaving a Legacy

Susan Bryant

In my role as a Financial Planner, I've been giving families advice for over 30 years. I've seen them all. Big ones, small ones and everything in between. The same goes for family businesses. Complex, straightforward - you name it.

The defining feature that shines bright from the most successful though, is clear and inspired leadership.

The role of a leader in a family or family business is complex. For me, ultimately it means being a visionary catalyst - defining, sharing and supporting the family vision to facilitate growth, both personally and professionally. The role of leadership is the key to enduring success; the aspects of how you lead will be the gift you leave behind and what others will say about you when you're gone. In other words, your Legacy.

As a family grows and diversifies, a talented leader displays stewardship. In a family business they can bring harmony to the various layers within the group and provide support to the incumbent business owner's vision for the business. Either from the inside or on the fringes, they can work towards building a sustainable business and family.

I spent nearly two decades living and working in a regional rural area of Australia, advising hundreds of farming families. I also spent nearly a decade, in both Sydney and Brisbane, Australia, working in Private Wealth Management with some of Australia's wealthiest, dynastic families. I learnt many lessons from both groups. I developed my practice towards working with family businesses and, specifically, with primary producers. Their sense of family and place is awe inspiring.

In those many years of working with families a couple of key things stood out.

Where there was a leadership vacuum, there followed in-fighting, strife, family breakdown, lost opportunity, fractured relationships and economic impact. Poor leadership is wealth destroying. These families' most dire fear was loss.

The most successful families, however, found strength from within. Under wise leadership they found a safe place to build resilience and share the load.

Crucial to this? A family leader must always nurture the vision about which all members should be clear. They should direct the legacy they have chosen to leave, and support others who may aspire to follow. This process of leadership works to bridge the seemingly impassable gap between the family business and non-business owners.

In fact, the most effective family leaders focus on three things. They are *Communication, Purpose*, and *Legacy*.

Communication

Start with *Communication.*

Sometimes this happens informally, in the yards working, perhaps, but if you really want it to be effective, formalise it. Send invitations, take minutes, circulate them - it's important absolutely everyone gets a seat at the table and a chance to be heard.

Make sure everyone knows their role. In a family this can be informal, or in a business more structured, with input and role descriptions from an HR expert.

Share your vision, often and everywhere. The more family

members are aware and exposed to the big vision driving it all, the more they are able to participate and the better the ownership. What comes out of this is always rich and rewarding.

Communicating well means your family is able to clearly articulate your specific and meaningful outcomes; those things that are important and will most likely require time and money to achieve. Your outcomes can be both hard and soft, but they must be clear and concise; the more detail the better.

These can then be monitored, measured and re-evaluated constantly. Are we on track? If we are not on track what do we need to do to get back on track? Lead these discussions with kindness and intention. It's not often you get an opportunity in life to influence and steward until death.

Purpose

Overriding what you do, is *Why you do it*. Understanding your family purpose is the headline.

Purpose or values are like a rally flag from the battlefields of old. When things get tough this is a point to gather at and remind yourself of why you are doing this. Whether you are aware or not, every decision you make is driven by your values.

Taking time to think this through and discover why your family values the things they do is an essential exercise to inform your leadership.

Making decisions and taking directions in life are then all made through this prism, ensuring that before the head is applied to a decision, the heart is fully in step with what's truly important to you. Failure to work through this step will ultimately result in incongruence and disharmony.

Relationships may be fractured, opportunities lost. Knowing what your family's most deeply held purpose and values are gives you an instant advantage and serves to pull you together when the going gets tough.

Large family businesses do this well. Over generations, they develop verbal and written agreements that address issues such as governance, structure, who can be on the board, what key decisions the board can make, including the appointment of the CEO, which family members can (or can't) work in the business, and edicts around philanthropy. The continual development and understanding of these agreements, and the governance decisions guided by them, may involve several kinds of family structures.

A family board representing different branches and generations of the family, for instance, may be responsible to a larger family group used to build consensus on major issues.

Family leaders can take a leaf from this corporate book and in a more informal way introduce some of these concepts within the family. By doing so you also leave a structure to ensure continuity.

Legacy

With courage and resilience you can then begin to build your *Legacy*. True legacy is more than just money. It is the continuity of family or family business.

Share your vision through story telling. Science has now proven that we remember stories way beyond the lecture. Our brains are hard wired to pay attention and recall both the emotions and the people, to recount later. Stories can bind generations together; distant and near family members can share something in common.

Taking the time to choose and craft your family story puts you in control of the lasting legacy you leave. In family business you can embed it into your entire decision making process and deliberately build it into your family business principles that build legacy around culture, protection of family respect and honour for all family members.

Work on a succession plan, make it open and transparent. Talk about it from when children are very young. This is the thread that pulls it all together. It may be that succession is as fair as it can be, but not equal. This can be a difficult concept if it's left to the last word (like a Will).

Ultimately my experience has shown that families who develop good communication, clear values and a worthy legacy are more likely to thrive during difficult family situations.

Research from the McKinsey Report shows one-third of all companies in the S&P 500 index and 40 percent of the 250 largest companies in France and Germany are defined as *family businesses.*

In Australia the fastest growing contributor to GDP is agri-business and of the 135,000 Australian farms, 99% are family owned.

Family businesses are the engine room of the Australian economy and employ more than 50% of the workforce. The peculiar and individual strengths of family are indisputable and family business is clearly an economic force. Leadership within those families is not just for kitchen table conversation anymore.

Family is at the heart of everything we hold dear. Family is the ideal incubator for innovation and new ideas if the leadership structure allows room for it. It's also the best place to grow good people. Get this right and you've given not only your own family a great gift but one from which others can benefit.

Working within your family to define leadership and nurture it in others can lead to the most profound outcomes.

Unsurprisingly, the traits you see in a successful family are pretty much those you would find in a good person.

When leadership is lacking or weak the results can be devastating. Decisions are avoided, deferred or made arbitrarily. There is no awareness and therefore no accountability, as the problem cannot be defined. Individuals, in an effort to protect themselves, turn on each other. Family heritage is destroyed and a different legacy is left - one of distrust, ridicule, even contempt. Not a legacy for which you would want to be known.

Anyone in a family can be a leader. It takes those three steps and when you bring that all together and focus on each one, your leadership creates a unique eco-system, a gift to your family and the world. Isn't that something worth being remembered for?

References

- Caspar. C. Dias. A.K. and Elstrodt. H-P. (2010) *The five attributes of enduring family businesses.* McKinsey and Company.

About Susan Bryant

Susan Bryant is an experienced and insightful financial planner. She specialises in working with Primary Producers with significant assets to build a legacy that ultimately leads to family harmony.

Susan has over 30 years in the Financial Planning profession, much of that time spent in Toowoomba, and more than a decade in private wealth management with industry leading Private Banks looking after wealthy dynastic families. She has a Diploma in Financial Service (Financial Planning) and is a Member of the Financial Planners Association (FPA).

Ultimately Susan's goal is change the way leading rural families think about having a plan for their future that is going to stand the test of time. Not just for them but for all the generations that will follow. It makes the hard work and the discomfort of *those* conversations worth all the effort. It's simply about creating deeper connections - to each other - to the past and to the future. And most importantly to ourselves.

Susan is an engaging and entertaining speaker. She regularly speaks at leading rural and regional industry conferences and has shared the stage with a snake at a Royal Flying Doctors community clinic.

Susan has presented a regular finance talk with Regional ABC radio, broadcast across western Queensland.

Website: www.seedsofadvice.com

Email: Susan@seedsofadvice.com

LinkedIn: http://au.linkedin.com/in/susanbryant1

Twitter: @ValuedAdviser

Facebook: @Seedsofadvice

Mindset

Psychology, motivation, development, experience, upbringing, self-talk, emotions, feelings, resilience, emotional intelligence, self-worth, perceived ability to control, mental health

Overcoming the Challenges
of the Modern Day CEO

Naeem Arif

The Modern Day CEO cuts a very different figure to what I grew up with. The mature male, in a suit and tie who has decades of experience and many qualifications, still exists, but is less common. We now associate the likes of Zuckerberg, Musk or maybe Ginni Rometty or Satya Nadella as CEO's of the leading modern brands. Not only can we see diversity in age, gender or ethnicity, but also we are seeing a very different set of experiences and capabilities.

Being a top CEO today is not just about what you have on your CV – it's about how you are able to deal within the modern world. So what are the characteristics that you need to develop to win as a Modern Leader? Having worked closely with many senior leaders in the last 20 years I have seen the good, bad and the ugly.

In this chapter I talk about the practical aspects that an MBA will not teach you and so give guidance on how you can meet the challenge of being a Modern Day CEO. There is a lot of talk around innovation, but this does not only mean technology, you can be innovative in your thinking and your culture as well.

Desire

Everyone talks about having the right mindset, in terms of having that winning mentality, that ability to work harder than everyone else. It is not by your effort, but by your strategy that you will really make a difference and here are two desires you need to build into your own DNA.

Firstly, when I say desire, I am talking about having the desire to do the right thing for your customers. Too many businesses are chasing financial targets, which may lead to short term success. For long-term success I am a firm believer that you need to be chasing satisfied customers. If you can get regular customer satisfaction, then the money will come itself.

Secondly, your successes and your failures; do you review and seek feedback as to what went well and what didn't? Some of the most successful CEO's are prepared to admit that they were wrong. They are willing to Pivot in a new direction when needed. It's not so important how you do it, but have the desire to reflect, learn and evolve your own performance. Feed these insights into your thinking and planning. Remember this is something

Learn from yesterday, live for today, hope for tomorrow.
The important thing is not to stop questioning - Albert Einstein

Maximising your current resources

In a world where it is always possible to get things cheaper and faster, how can you maximise the assets within your organisation? Well simply by looking after that important asset that is unique to you; your people.

We should all consider ourselves to be in the *People2People* business and treat our people like we want them to treat our customers. If you can ensure your employees are happy, then they will take that happiness into their interactions with your customers.

*If you take care of your Employees, they will take care
of your Clients - Richard Branson*

As a CEO, your role should be to create an environment of high performing people and there are a couple of key ways in which organisations can do this; Hiring the right people and empowering them to get on with it. Don't hire people like you, hire people better than you. Give them enough opportunity to add their own personal inputs (within the culture and values of your organisation) and see how this can create something special for the whole organisation.

*Hire people who are better than you and then leave them
to get on with it - David Ogilivy*

Externally, build your network of influencers and partners, as this can become a valuable asset for you. Who you are spending time with is going to shape your own thinking. Seek out people who can elevate your thinking and your brand. You need to think about building a network, not just to sell your product, but to learn about other people and their problems. These interactions will give you ideas and opportunities to work together in a partnership that will create value for both parties.

Risk Appetite

Taking risks is an essential part of business because playing it safe will often make you another *me-too* organisation. With over 700 new businesses setting up every day in the UK, you can easily be left behind if you do not take chances.

This is not about being foolish, it is about taking risks in proportion to the rewards that you are trying to achieve. The best way to do this is to take a risk based approach to every decision you are going to make.

If you really want to stand out, you need to think about taking some risks in terms of your branding, positioning and your target market. Whilst it maybe easy to do more of the same, *evolving how we do things today* is important in order to keep satisfying your customers.

Be Commercially Focussed

What does this mean? Well put quite simply it is an understanding of how every action you do will generate revenue. Many CEO's get so caught up in marketing or positioning that they lose focus on making sales. Without losing the Customer Satisfaction aspect, this is about ensuring that your actions are linking back to a revenue opportunity, in the short, medium or long term.

Without customers you don't have a business, so any business that does not pay attention to its customers will not be in business for a long time. The trap many fall into is to think that everyone is your customer. That's a massive challenge even for Nike or Coca Cola to achieve and so they all focus on a specific market and don't try to be everything for everyone.

The Modern Day CEO knows this and focuses on a target market who they can satisfy best. Being able to ignore market segments is an important commercial decision to make and allows you to focus on your target market even more. Some of the best commercial decisions are around knowing who you are and what you are not.

Become the leader even you would follow

If people are your best assets, then retaining your people is often a key part of winning. Organisations that look after their employees, find that in return, their employees look after their customers. There is a difference between Leadership and Management. Unfortunately many people do not understand the difference between the two.

These are not exclusive skills, but you should be able to know when to Lead or when to Manage.

A great manager is memorable because of their ability to get people to do their jobs. They are often all-rounders, not particularly amazing at anything other than being organised and able to pull things together.

A great leader is memorable because of their ability to get people to follow them. They are often inspirational or revolutionary in some areas and can sometimes create something inspiring and magical for their customers.

If you can get people to follow you to the ends of the earth, you are a great leader - Indra Nooyi

Being authentic in the way you approach leading or managing is important. Create your own style, which is based upon your personality because that will be something you will be able to maintain in the long term. Just because you read about Steve Jobs or Mark Zuckerberg does not mean their style is right for you.

Don't be afraid to delegate to people in your team who can handle the responsibility. It speeds up delivery, also develops your people, which will in the future lead to more opportunities for your business.

The term *Lead by example* is often misleading for some people and they instead get *The Hero Syndrome* as I call it. They feel that everything is now their responsibility; they have to get out there and do everything, make every decision or make every sale.

Being able to Lead does not mean that you have to do all the action, good leaders tend to step up when they need to, when there is a gap in the delivery. Allow your team the opportunity to be part of the delivery as well as the decision-making. You will find that they have a lot of creativity in them and your role should be to allow that to come to fruition.

Finally, celebrate the success of the group as a group, but be ready to stand up as the leader when things are not going to well. Leaders come to the front, when they are needed the most.

In times of great difficulty, when you look around your organisation, the leaders will appear. - Naeem Arif

Summary
Being a CEO in the Modern Age is difficult considering the rate of change we are experiencing. The world will continue to evolve and grow, so be prepared to do the same. Your role in this is to deal with the changes and pivot your own thinking and strategy, in a timely manner, to deal with this evolving environment.

As CEO, it is your duty to develop both your organisation and your people. Creating an environment where your team can express themselves is both beneficial to your organisation and rewarding for your team, leading to a better result all around.

The most important thing to take away from this chapter is that if you're worried that you were not born with it, don't worry, you can develop yourself into an effective CEO by doing these simple things right. It's not just about what you do, but about what you can create with the right people around you.

About Naeem Arif

Over the last 20 years, Naeem has provided Management Consultancy services to CEO's, Directors and the Senior Leaders of major corporations globally. A key skill he has developed is to not only manage complex projects but also work with demanding stakeholders.

He has completed more than 18 Corporate Transformation projects for global brands and at the same time he is the CEO of his own Retail business, building it up from a blank canvas into a major retail operation in Birmingham. It is this combination of Consulting and Business Ownership that makes Naeem stand out from other the Business Executives on the market.

As CEO of NA Consulting, Naeem has built a team that is transforming Entrepreneurs into thriving CEO's. Naeem is at his best, when developing strategies that focus on the Customer. Creating satisfied customers is the best way to retain your customers and customer retention is the most profitable business strategy you can adopt in relation to capital expenditure.

https://www.linkedin.com/in/naeemarif/

Twitter: @NAConsultingLtd

Website: www.NAConsulting.co.uk

YouTube: NA Consulting Ltd

Email: Info@NAConsulting.co.uk

Human-Centred Leadership Mindset

Dr Kylie Hutchings Mangion
CAHRI EdD MEdTech BLDes (USQ) BTeach (PAVE) (CQU)

You have significant influence in your role as a leader, and how you wield that influence can and will impact the outcome of your teams' effort. Positive or negative, your actions, behaviours and words contribute to your worker's performance, regardless of the leadership style you display. Further, while there are many leadership development programs available on virtually every human resource subject, at the end the day, it's up to you to inspire and guide your team members to achieve their highest level of productivity on a daily basis.

Despite misconceptions about the concept, a human-centred approach to corporate leadership is appropriate in every workplace setting. When you understand how and why the performance of your workers affects your ultimate organisational goals, you can optimise those outcomes by aligning the tasks and environment to enable rather than inhibit the employee's performance. The aim here is to assist you to grasp where to start the process of unleashing your team's full potential. Your workers are by far the most valuable asset of your organisation and therefore, your most valuable asset. Leaders who don't recognise or acknowledge this reality are simply missing out on the opportunity to achieve true corporate greatness, and frankly, are undermining the ultimate purpose behind actual leadership.

Understanding the full scope of human-centred work practice can be an extensive endeavour, which is typical of all studies related to human factors and cognitive ergonomics. However, don't let this barrier cause you to avoid your journey toward closing the gap between you and your people.

All leaders begin their workforce development process by first developing their personal leadership skills, and from there, they are much better able to align themselves with their worker resource.

Once the leader is truly engaged and engaging with the workers at their prime level, it is absolutely possible to both deliver on organisational goals, objectives, obligations and accountabilities while embracing a more human-centred approach to team management. As a result of your personal effort to become the best leader possible, you will not only deliver optimal outcomes for your company, but the enhanced collaboration with your staff will help them to achieve higher levels of satisfaction and productivity than they have previously experienced.

Your development journey begins by understanding two separate but related concepts, each of which is based on our fundamental human experiences:

- the human *cognitive* state - how we think, and
- the human *affective* state - how we feel.

These *Human Principles* provide a scaffold for developing a human-centred approach to leadership. You first explore the concepts within your own role as a leader, and then you can explore how these concepts affect your workers. A few easy-to-implement strategies are all you need to get started in developing and shifting your mindset to embrace a more productive leadership style. From there, by engaging a few simple changes to how you engage with each of your workers, you can unlock volumes of as-yet untapped human resources.

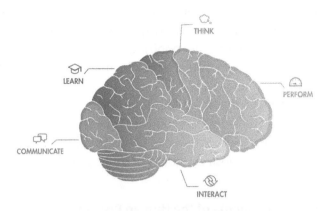

Figure 1: The Human Principle

The Human Principle

Before we begin to look at the key elements of *The Human Principle*, you must recognize that this approach to leadership requires letting go of past, less productive management practices. If your current leadership style has a high level of control, it's time to soften those edges. This does not mean that you are relinquishing your role or the impact you can have on your workforce. *The Human Principle* approach is about assisting you to achieve and deliver, not avoid or delegate any level of your role's accountability.

To get started, you'll need to understand where you stand now in relation to the elements of the Human Principles:

- Assess and acknowledge your current leadership practices - how you approach your workforce now;

- Then identify the effect that your current practices have on them, and

- Then contemplate how these behaviours can be altered in future.

Note that the insights you gain will not require huge changes immediately. An important aspect of your own personal leadership development is recognizing that you are dealing with people and, should you attempt to make changes that seem out of sync, illogical or even worse non-genuine, your attempts to redirect them will fail. Your unexpected changes may even have an adverse effect on your staff and might cause irrevocable damage. Remember, the aim is to become a more effective leader, not to lose credibility or insult your people.

The Elements of the Human Principle

Think

The first element is THINK, and the key subtopic we have extracted for THINK is *self-efficacy*. The notion of self-efficacy pertains to how each worker gauges their capacity to do the work. Individuals with a strong concept of self-efficacy will see most tasks as doable and easily assume those challenges. People with a less developed sense of self-efficacy may determine that, for them, a task is unachievable and that determination can increase their stress and promote their failure. As a leader, how can you encourage and nurture your people's internal "can do" gauge and increase their self-efficacy capacity?

Learn

The second element is LEARN, and the key subtopic we have extracted for LEARN is *content prioritisation*. Knowing how to prioritise incoming information is a critical skill for every worker because they are often flooded with information that exhausts their cognitive resources. Many feel *time-poor,* and simply scan information rather than effectively processing it. These cursory scans, however, often miss important information and without that informational directive, workers often experience poor results.

As the leader in your instructional space, your projects should include an initial phase of knowledge prioritisation to ensure that your staff don't simply scan incoming data without capturing its significance, including its potential impact on workflows. When they understand what to look for, your team can extract the core content needed from the raw content collected from subject matter experts.

Assessing Your Staff

So, now you have an insight on two key topic areas of *The Human Principle,* and you can evaluate the affective states of your team members through these two lenses. To gain the most accurate perspective, you must know what they think and how they feel. Many leaders assume that they know how their people feel and think. That assumption, however, defeats this process and is potentially detrimental to the productivity of the workforce in the long run.

How you approach your staff is also an important component of the process. Your approach will set the tone for the project and its success will lie in their receptiveness to your presentation and demeanour.

Consider these two possible approaches:

- Focus on your team's current structure of relationships and level of trust; or
- Maintain the company's previous track record of managing change.

Once you've determined which path works best in your situation, you can then choose one of two methods to gain the information you seek: either interview each worker or provide them with the opportunity to complete an empathetic map. In either case, be sure to use a consistent format, so the data collected is the same regardless of the method you choose.

Face-to-face meetings

Whether you are meeting one-on-one or in a group, keep the atmosphere informal and relaxed to encourage the most honest responses to your questions. Assure them that your inquiry isn't adversarial but an attempt to improve your work as their leader. Again, it's the style of the presentation and the track record of the company that will help or hinder this process.

Also, let your team know that you appreciate who they are, the effort they bring and their role as a team member. You want to understand how, as a team member, their work tasks and co-workers affect their ability to do their job. Share with them that the insights you gain are to help you to become a better leader and not to be used as a performance evaluation tool. It is crucial that you communicate to them that ultimate goal of this project if you want them fully onboard with the process.

Whether one-on-one or in a group, be sure to let them express themselves fully, either by speaking up or by contributing their information on a whiteboard alongside the comments of their co-workers. The key here is to enable a little creativity and allow the process to engage your team, yet avoid having them feel negated, opposed or unduly influenced by the other team members.

Use an Empathetic Map

Empathetic maps are valuable especially when you're concerned about the reception by your workers of the assessment project. The purpose of the empathetic map is to reveal how people feel about their work - their tasks, requests, social contexts or the work environment. The key to the map is to focus its questions to identify the areas that generate the most concern and therefore may also offer the best opportunity for positive growth. Those areas of concern will form the basis of your questions for your staff.

Gather Clarifying Information

No matter how you choose to gather the data, the information you are looking to unveil is the same: both the positive and negative aspects of both feelings and thought processes about the work.

You can enhance your workers contribution by having them suggest alternative scenarios, or by letting them write a new ending. This *extending* not only encourages future thinking but also allows team members the autonomy of contributing to a more positive workflow. After they've completed the extending exercise, ask them how they feel about the newly amended task or situation and let them explain why they made the changes.

Also inquire about how each worker responds to management requests. How each team member *hears* a request can dramatically shape how they react to it, both ositively and negatively. If the worker has a negative response to a request, it could be because the request is phrased with a negative connotation, which can be off-putting or even threatening. Learning to present requests to elicit positive responses and higher engagement is a quick and easy way to make adjustments to how those messages are received.

Ultimately, you are seeking to discover how your people react in response to a range of given tasks, situations and environments. By taking the time to contextualize your questions to your specific work environment, you'll gather more information that is relevant to the goals you seek.

Applying elements and key topics from *The Human Principle* together with an empathetic profiling map of key team members will provide you with a foundation from which you can move forward in further developing yourself as an influential leader.

About Dr Kylie Hutchings Mangion

Dr Kylie Hutchings Mangion is a Cognitive Ergonomist and the Executive Director of *Human CKOde*. As an expert in human cognitive performance, she specialises in human-centred leadership and design. Her flagship executive mentorship program helps Human Resource Leaders master the Art of Employee Retention.

She has over 25 years' experience in learning and development, and the concept of instructional design and development under sound leadership management is at the core of her passion of how humans construct knowledge.

Dr Kylie Hutchings Mangion is also an Academic for Charles Sturt University and lectures across all faculties and within the Schools of Information Studies, Education, Graduate Policing and Biomedical Sciences, sharing with both faculty and students her extensive knowledge in the areas of cognitive processing, communications and human-centred practices. In the commercial setting, psychosocial and cognitive ergonomic principles from a human factors perspective form the basis of her focus, and she provides industry leaders with the necessary insights to optimise the human experience within their organisation's areas of leadership, design, capacity and performance.

Dr Kylie Hutchings Mangion

CAHRI EdD MEdTech BLDes (USQ) BTeach (PAVE) (CQU)

Human CKODE

www.humanckode.com.au

kylie@humanckode.com.au

https://www.linkedin.com/in/dr-kylie-hutching-mangion/

Twitter: DrKHutchingsMangion @KHMTweets

Peak Performance (Your Role)

Ches Moulton

This article enables readers to look closely at their roles and what their responsibilities are in the workplace and the identification of skills, knowledge and attitude necessary to successfully develop themselves and their company.

Introduction

The old model of work-life balance that spoke to the division of time and effort between career and recreation, has been outdated and somewhat irrelevant for many years. The model that champions the vision of this formula in the 21st century, has become more about the quality of life related to levels of satisfaction and enjoyment, contrasted with stress and anxiety experienced by individuals.

Who we are at home, the levels of anxiety and happiness, our fears and phobias, our learned behaviour patterns and the forces that compel us in our relationship building skills, are the very same elements that we carry with us into our working environment. While some aspects of our workplace personna are uniquely exhibited in that environment, our underlying nature represents the foundation of the person we are, the manner in which we conduct ourselves and the way in which we interact with others during our daily work activities.

With this in mind, emphasis must be placed on addressing the emotional and mental compass and well being of individuals to ensure an equitable approach to all of the elements required for a balanced, happy, and productive employee intent on successful outcomes both professionally and personally.

Do I have a J.O.B. or a Career?

A job is an activity, often regular, and often performed in exchange for monetary considerations. A person usually begins a job by becoming an employee or volunteering. If a person is trained for a certain type of task, it may be considered a profession. To many people, the daily or weekly expenditure of energy, necessary to provide a monetary income, is merely a means to an end. Many people within a workforce possess little or no motivation to become absorbed in their work life and consider their non-working hours to be the highest priority in their life. A job can be routine, boring and uninspiring, lacking creativity and flexibility and often short-term. As a result, there is no significant long-term emotional or mental attachment.

Career is defined by the Oxford English Dictionary as a person's "course or progress through life (or a distinct portion of life)". In this definition, career is understood to relate to a range of aspects of an individual's life, learning, and work.

*Caree*r is a word often used to describe the working aspect of an individuals life. The term career is also used to describe an occupation or a profession that usually involves special training or formal education, and is considered to be a person's lifework. In this case a career is seen as a sequence of related jobs usually pursued within a single industry or sector e.g. *a career in law*. Individuals who consider themselves in relation to having a career, are those people who are to some greater measure, involved in their work, have a moving set of goals and are in most instances, self motivated to achieve the highest level of accomplishment open to them.

Success in a career will be measured by the willingness to embrace change with a view toward finding solutions to problems and the level of achievement experienced.

Developing a multitude of transferrable skills will enhance your marketability and enable you to take advantage of and enjoy new and varied opportunities.

Establish your own meaning for work and fit it in with the realities of the external demands placed on you. Deciding whether you want a job or career can sometimes depend on where you are in your life cycle and the priorities you have. How you view work and the connection to life determines whether you have a job or a career.

What life skills do I bring to my work?

By the time an individual becomes involved in the workforce, he or she would have obtained certain life skills that can be essential in acquiring and maintaining a position. These include but are not limited to personal, interpersonal, communication, and presentation skills with a basic aptitude in writing and numeracy. The degree to which an individual has or can develop these skills can be a determining factor in the level of achievement which will experienced.

Individuals seeking opportunities to experience higher levels of achievement will possess and excel in decision making and problem solving skills. Organisational skills and project and change management skills are imperative for people who aspire to successful leadership. Great leaders also exhibit exceptional speaking and effective listening skills along with negotiation and organisational abilities.

What is my role? Does it serve me, my colleagues, company, and customers?

A key factor getting in the way of individual, group and organisational success is a lack of role clarity. Role clarity is one of the critical challenges faced by employees in the modern economy and it is an even bigger problem for organisations. It is difficult for an organisation to be successful when clear alignment between its objectives and what people spend time doing is blurred or non-existent

Obstacles To Role Clarity

Lack of clear objectives

A job description is often a litany of tasks and responsibilities. A realistic statement of expected outcomes people can use to prioritise and organise their efforts is a document more consistent with defining clear and achievable performance outcomes.

An example is an administrative professional who does everything asked of him but continues to receive feedback from customers indicating he isn't *doing his job*.

Clearly a disconnect exists in terms of expectations. It is quite probable the job description looks a lot more like the list of tasks he is doing than it does a statement of the outcomes his customers are expecting.

Lack of communication

Communication is the cornerstone of every successful relationship. Unquestionably people don't invest enough time communicating about the right things. Too many resources are spent on meetings, developing strategies and problem solving. Leaders spend very little time communicating about context, priorities and expectations and employees fail to ask for help. They hesitate to ask questions about what is expected of them.

They fear that seeking clarification in prioritising activities and decisions will make them look incompetent. So they continue to stumble along in the dark on their own.

As an employee, arrest your ego, set aside your misgivings and seek answers to the questions that trouble you. Don't assume it is your duty alone to determine what your responsibilities are. When in doubt, ask. And even when you think you get it, ask anyway. You might be surprised by what you hear. The answers to your questions might provide you with feedback on your performance and indicate the broader thinking of management as it relates to the bigger picture.

The manifestation of role clarity is relatively simple. As an employee it is important to know that when seeking assistance and direction, it is useful to frame the conversation in a manner that shows interest in the successful outcomes of expended efforts and an interest in sustaining a high level of dignity, integrity and job satisfaction. A healthy and productive environment both individually and collectively is directly related to the sense of accomplishment one has in their contribution to the success of the company.

As a leader, set expectations early, and revisit them often. Time spent connecting job responsibilities to broader goals and objectives of the team and organisation is an invaluable expenditure of resources. Regular meetings with team members ought to be a priority. Leadership isn't something to do when there isn't anything to occupy your time. If it is, you might want to re-visit your own job description and expectations.

Your Responsibility At Work

A challenge that many individuals face once they have been employed for a length of time, usually for a year or two and are focusing on the next step in their career advancement, begin looking for what the organisation can offer in the future.

The path to promotion can present many obstacles, many of which cannot be controlled. Let's focus on the things that can be managed, ensuring personal as well as professional development goals can be attained.

An examination of the different stages of employment is essential for familiarisation of potential roadblocks and their inhibiting affect.

In the first stage of work life, most employees are an individual contributor, working either dependently or independently and rely on others and the business organisation.

If you are working independently, it is necessary to be alert. Ensure you are not inhibiting both your personal and professional development.

Be certain to have initiative, show a willingness to get involved in group projects, demonstrate the ability to focus on more than one task and simultaneously work on multiple projects, always leading to successful outcomes. For individuals working in a group or team surrounding, some of the challenges may include a heightened competitive environment, or an inability to build relationships with colleagues.

Successful navigation through this first stage of work life opens the door to the next challenge as you begin to make a contribution through the efforts of others.

Delegate responsibilities to others, while selling your ideas and concepts to other groups in the organisation. At this stage in your career, you will want to think about the bigger picture and the needs of the organisation, as well as your own department. Some supervisors feel threatened by employees that are ambitious and successful. Having someone who can one day replace you will make it easier to move up in the organisation.

During the final stage the opportunity arrives to contribute throughout the entire organisation.

It is at this time in a person's career that the understanding and awareness gained from personal growth will pay dividends as you move closer to the upper levels of the organisation. Challenges often faced in this role include scenarios such as completing projects on budget and developing time management skills.

Building relationships and networks with others in the company is essential for successful outcomes.

It becomes obvious there are many obstacles on the ascending journey up the corporate ladder. In order to help your career, it is important to seek out and become involved in employee and personal development training programmes. As you gain more responsibility, you will be tasked with making sure your colleagues and subordinates receive the best employee training and development available.

Your credibility will surge if you have experienced classes, seminars and learning in the past, prior to helping guide your staff through their career development process.

By establishing an opportunity to improve people's skills, it is possible to maximise personal development within your organisation and solidify your role as a leader.

About Ches Moulton

Ches Moulton specialises in working with executives who suffer from stress and dysfunctional relationships. His business is designed to help people acquire a skill set, enabling them to improve their lives through a greater awareness of who they are and how and why they became the type of person they have grown into being.

Currently, Ches manages a successful private practice and since 1999 has designed, developed and delivered mental skills training programmes for business leaders resulting in less stress, more confidence, and increased clarity and creativity

He is the author of the International Bestseller *'Choice & Change - How to have a healthy relationship with ourself and others'.*

Working internationally since 1994, Ches has successfully raised awareness to executives of the need to modify their thoughts, emotions, and behaviour to the people, places, and things that impact them on a daily basis!

An engaging public speaker he has been featured in the media including BBC, Essentials Magazine and at high-level presentations in Canada, the Caribbean, United Kingdom, the Middle East and Africa.

Ches is redefining the way in which people view their environment leaving them feeling liberated and confident about their future.

Website: chesmoulton.com
Youtube: Ches Moulton
LinkedIn: Ches Moulton
Twitter: @chesmoulton
Facebook: Helping People Achieve More

Mindfulness: The Antidote for Burnout Leaders

Tony Jeton Selimi

As leaders, all too often we lose track of what is most important to us. Consciously or unconsciously we get distracted and pulled into the surrounding chaos. As a consequence, rather than focus and face into matters that are left unattended, we start to feel as though this is the norm leaders are meant to follow.

Deep down we notice a barrage of emotions such as frustration, anger, anxiety, and a feeling of not being good enough. Yet, more and more, we are becoming immune to such life-threatening stressors that our body's inner ALARM is trying to alert us to.

We continue to work long hours, work under tremendous pressure, and we give in to all sort of addictions that further cultivate the environment under which burnout loves to thrive. Insomnia, stress, and anxiety start to impact our personal and professional lives. We start to make ethical mistakes, bad choices, and decisions that lead to loss of productivity. And that is just the tip of what more is hidden beneath the iceberg that burnout represents.

Regrettably, in many companies across the world where I have been asked to tackle all sort of performance, lack of productivity, and profitability issues, I notice a growing trend of working long hours to be something that everyone should brag about. But, leaders and employees alike barely blink an eye on the impact and the true cost of burnout.

It is true that many leaders work in places where high pressure working environments are the norm, but this attitude of praising long hours as a sign of a person working hard, of going above and beyond, has extremely damaging long-term consequences that span over a prolonged period of time.

Many of the Fortune 500 executives that have sought my help were blindly following this trend that stops them from leading with the kind of excellence that deep down they knew they were capable of exhibiting. On a deeper inspection and through powerful questioning, they come to realize the personal and professional impact of this day-to-day autopilot existence.

Some felt as though they are hopeless, barely having the energy to make it through the day, and others shared how they've lost their passion, joy, and motivation. Uniformly, due to the ever-increasing family demands, pressures, and expectations, they felt they needed to work longer hours whilst watching life passing them by.

Not being present for every moment of our life is not common just to high achievers, in fact, it is everyone's problem derived from living in a day an age where we are constantly expected to live our lives being distracted. And, when you are distracted, there is no chance that you can lead with the kind of excellence it is expected of you as a leader of your own life, your relationship, a classroom, a team, or an organization.

According to 2017 UK government's Health, Safety and Executive report, 1 in 3 employees expect to burnout on the job, which makes job burnout more common than getting the flu. Unlike flue that can last few weeks, burnout has much longer-term negative effects that if unattended, it can lead to chronic illness, depression, and in worst case scenario to suicide.

Leadership burnout is a real problem that in one shape or form is affecting millions of people across the globe.

The interesting thing is, if you pay attention, no matter where you go, no matter whom you are, people across the world time and time again say words like "I'm so exhausted, I am stressed, I am tired, I need a break, I need a cigarette, I need a holiday, I have a headache, I don't need sex, I just need a good night sleep, yet barely anyone questions themselves or others what are they are truly saying when we use such words.

Truth is, if we pay attention, listening carefully, we will come to understand how our body's intelligence is communicating to us through its inbuilt ALARM about the things that keep us continually frazzled.

There are many definitions for burnout that you can read more about, that said, let me share with you my definition: Burnout is a stressed induced state of vital exhaustion that leads to psychosomatic erosion.

Mental, emotional, and physical exhaustion can lead to psychosomatic erosion often found among highly motivated people who work in mentally, emotionally and physically demanding jobs. When this happens, you are no longer able to function effectively on a personal, professional or business level.

The common mistake I have seen many leaders make is that they think burnout is something that happens suddenly. Truth is, no one wakes up one morning and all of a sudden has a burnout. Its nature is much more deceptive, sneaking up on us over time like a slow gas leak, which makes it much harder for any of us to diagnose.

Despite the dangers overachiever syndrome that leads to burnout represents, I found that many leaders often prioritize what's expected of them above the warnings of their body's innate ALARM mechanism.

Let's just imagine you are with a group in front of a steep, almost vertical cliff that you are all asked to climb. Not each one of you may feel is courageous enough to do it.

This is because each one of you will measure, analyze and anticipate your aptitudes according to your individual abilities, perceived limits, and beliefs. Some of the people in the group will say I can do it, they will start climbing the cliff, but eventually only a few of them make the way to the top of the cliff. Other members of the group will try repetitively to climb the cliff without any significant outcome and they end up either inundated or precipitated with cliff debris.

Similarly, numerous leaders in the corporate world experience burnout not because they cannot climb their professional ladder, but because they cannot stay steady while carrying an overwhelming burden of seemingly unsurmountable working engagements.

Having coached and mentored hundreds of high achievers, I conclude that burnout amongst leaders is not likely to be brought up by one particular problem, but by the accumulative result of multiple stressors that add up over the period of time.

Due to effects of burnout, many executives no longer listen to the messages of their inner ALARM, instead they leave those messages unattended. When it starts buzzing, then a whole range of signs will commence alarming our mind and body that the onset of burnout is on our doorstep.

As mentioned before, burnout is a state of vital exhaustion, a state where you feel energetically drained of your life force. At the start, as high achiever leaders, we try to compensate by camouflaging ourselves saying that there is nothing to be worried about.

But in the long run, this ignorance of our true inner state is what creates dire psychosomatic repercussions. One poignant example of this is when we try to deceive ourselves that we can cope by consistently denying to face the real problem.

This is what eventually lead towards the emergence of emotional, cognitive and physical exhaustion, depletion of work performance and impaired work-life balance.

To be stressed out at work is a common practice and therefore we tend to drop our defense mechanism and we stop paying too much attention to it.

But once the Cortisol level starts to surge, our inner ALARM (Hypothalamus) will alter our intrinsic homeostasis. As a result, we might wake up one particular morning with resentment towards the people, situations, and the work we used to adore until yesterday.

We don't seem as the leaders who once had the same stamina and energy. In contrary, you might end up being like a leader you have never wanted to be like and more and more you start to feel incapable of executing choices, decisions, and effectively performing at work.

This is what is known as chronic fatigue, a state which entails: lack of energy, emotional exhaustion, and torpid mental performance. Gradually, despite the working overload you will end up staring blank at your desk papers and feel frustrated, anxious and powerless. This state of ineffectiveness and lack of accomplishment could lead to depression, isolation, and social detachment.

You try to avoid breaks with your colleagues, your sexual arousal is declining, and you end feeling alienated from your family. This feeling of helplessness and hopelessness is what is causing multiple sleepless nights and disruption of REM and non-REM phase of our regular sleep patterns.

Insomnia, in turn, might give rise to ADD, CDD, and severe impairment in concentration, poor focus and slow cognitive tempo. These problems are leading to one detrimental outcome which is a deflated financial portfolio in the corporate sector. Once the financial security of your business is impaired, you are less likely to be a desirable leader.

To support you on this journey, here are *Five TJS Mindfulness Principles* you can use to equip yourself with the antidote needed to spot, address and avoid leadership burnout.

1. Acknowledge your power by transforming distractions into dedicated actions. Focus on what's highest in the priority of your values, prioritize those activities, and delegate the rest. This will free up the time needed to maximize your productivity at work whilst maintaining work-life balance.

2. Learn to Love the unlovable. Mindfully chose to respond to your internal negative self-talk and external judgments by practicing the art of gratitude. Put your self-love and your well-being first. You are no good to anyone if you yourself are indisposed, make a conscious choice to invite love to encapsulate and lead your being. Take time for yourself and make sure you find opportunities within the busy work schedule to take more frequent though short breaks.

3. Strive to achieve self-mastery. Getting in touch with your highest expression of yourself is what will help you listen to your inner truth. You can do so by daily feeding your mind with the knowledge that can support you to lead your inner being.

4. Move from reasons and resistance to Results driven Vision. As the famous saying goes, those who fail to plan, fail to achieve. Being disorganized is what steals your most precious asset-time. Consciously chose to plan your days, months, and years in alignment with your highest purpose.

5. Allow the Miracle that life is to guide you in every area of life. Nature is a perfect teacher as well as an oasis where you can escape when the tough gets going. Daily set 30 minutes time in your diary to meditate, in doing so, you maximize your frontal cortex capabilities. The way you chose to respond towards anyone who challenges your core values, consciously or unconsciously becomes mindful.

Lastly, remember, burnout is a cumulative result of the choices and decisions you make in every moment of your awakening life. Use the above five principles to merge your inner leader with kinesthetic intelligence to energize teams, boost productivity, and achieve a healthy work-life balance.

About Tony Jeton Selimi

Tony Jeton Selimi is considered to be among world's leading authorities on assisting people to achieve quantum leaps in empowering all of key areas of life, including social, business, finances, spiritual, physical, relationship, mental and emotional well-being.

His work is embraced by *Fortune 500* CEO's, entrepreneurs, MP's, royalty, billionaires, and global influencers.

With more than 20+ years' experience in business and in information technology, Tony teaches leaders and organizations how to mindfully engage, empower and elevate people thus inspiring action that increases performance, productivity, profits, people's vitality, and helps them move forward with confidence.

Based on this *TJS Evolutionary Method: ALARM*™ framework and his own life's transformation, he then wrote the #1 International best-selling books *A Path to Wisdom* and award winning *#Loneliness*, and co-created *Living My Illusion*, a multi award-winning real life coaching documentary, which instantly have become a global phenomenon.

His talks inspire audiences globally, including the stages of the UN, Cranfield School of Management, *London Business Show*, and *TEDx*. Appearances on Radio and TV stations across the world include interviews by Jack Canfield and Brian Tracy on *SKY, ABC, NBC, CBS, FOX* and *News 24* reaching over 50 million viewers worldwide.

For further information:

http://tonyselimi.com

LinkedIn: https://www.linkedin.com/in/tonyselimi/

Social/Relationships

Quality of life, quality of experience, quality of environment, connection to family, friends, community, work, social, relationships, stress

Conversations That Flow

Matthew Newnham

"I've learned that people will forget what you said, people will forget what you did, but people will never forget how you made them feel." Maya Angelou

When was the last time you were in a conversation about something significant that flowed so well that you all had a reaction something along these lines, "Wow, what an excellent conversation **that** was! That felt **great!**"

If you've had a conversation like this recently, great. If you experience them frequently, fantastic. (And congratulations - you're in a small minority.) On the other hand, if this isn't your experience, you're not alone.

I'd like to share with you the one thing that I have found makes the biggest difference if you want to have more of these *Conversations That Flow*, more often and with less effort and stress. This is based on years of practical experience with people from all walks of life around the world.

P.S. One final thing before we move on: I'm not really interested in conversations where directives are issued via one-way announcements. Those aren't conversations; they're broadcasts. By default, they invite resistance and dissent more often than not. However, what I'm about to share can be used to improve even these 'conversations'.

"I Know Just What You're Thinking"

In the marketing world, that line has been used endless times by copywriters. How does the marketing person (or your well-meaning friend trying to console you, for that matter) "know exactly what you're thinking"? How presumptuous! And anyway, who wants to be seen as that predictable?

In my experience of studying conversations for as long as I can remember, most of the ones that are beset by friction or stagnation get into that state because at least one party has already reached their own preconceived conclusions. And those conclusions are invariably based largely on what they think they know about the other person.

We all know why this isn't healthy; it's just an incredibly easy trap to fall into. On the other hand, some conversations falter because they get stuck in a different way: we feel that we have very little to go on when it comes to understanding and relating to the other people in the conversation.

In both cases, we have a failure to connect, based on a lack of understanding of the other person. And that's an invitation for friction, resistance, stuckness and stagnation to step in and stymie the conversation.

"Your Jedi Mind Tricks Won't Work On Me"

Conversations that flow need to meet the other person where they are, even if that's not always easy to do. To address this challenge, most of us have been on a reasonable amount of training or done some self-study on how to communicate effectively in the workplace. But how well is that working in practice?

It's quite something to step back and consider how many business conversations are designed to 'handle' the other person and get them to agree with your agenda. On the one hand, we all need to achieve progress.

However, here's a simple litmus test:

If we tried our various sales skills, presentation skills, negotiating skills etc on our family and closest friends for a month or so, how long do you think they'd put up with us?

In my experience, that doesn't go down very well! (Unless it's done as a parody, of course.)

That being the case, what makes us think that those (largely artificial) ways of conversing are the best way to create *Conversations That Flow* about things that matter? Given basic human psychology, I wouldn't bet on that.

What if we could find a more natural way of connecting meaningfully with others, so that we can have genuine conversations that flow and reach even better answers that we can all buy into? Even if it worked just a little better, wouldn't that be worth trying?

Your Natural Gateway to Connecting With Others

Over 3,500 years ago, the ancient Chinese noted that everything, and every person, has their own unique blend of five energy types, one for each time of the year.

This system of observation - built up over centuries - proved so powerful that it was used to manage their agriculture, conduct their commerce and govern their kingdom.

So how does this help you connect more meaningfully with others, so that you can have more *Conversations That Flow*, more often and with less effort?

Well, have you ever noticed how people who are truly comfortable in their own skin can operate with a calm sense of clarity and generous curiosity that puts others at ease?

That's what we find people can increasingly access, once they get to see themselves and others via their unique blend of *Five Energies*.

We have found that for most of us, the more we understand, the more compassionate and kind we tend to be. And that starts with ourselves. When we understand what's really informing how we operate, it's almost inevitable that we become kinder and more compassionate with ourselves and others.

This causes us to relax and be less attached to specific outcomes and more open to options. Just this shift alone can lead to a marked improvement in how well our conversations flow, both the ones we have within our own mind, and with others.

Which of The Five Energies Resonates Most With You?

Each Energy Type has characteristics (focus areas) drawn from one season of the year. In addition to these focus areas, each Energy Type also has a 'Big Question' that runs continuously on autopilot for each of us, day and night, consciously or unconsciously.

Once we are aware of our energy mix and what that entails for us, we are more awake to its potential, and we're more open to creative options on how to maximise it.

Here is a quick summary of each *Energy Type*. Which one(s) feel most like you?

Energy Type	Related Season	Selected Focus Areas and 'Big Question'
Water	Winter	Safety, risks (seeing and managing), consequences, sustainability, resources, history, purpose/legacy
		"Am I safe?" or *"Are we safe?"*

Wood	Spring	Creativity, vision, control, chaos, rules, boundaries, problem solving, tension, rigidity, release and justice
		"Am I free?" or *"Are we free?"*
Fire	Summer	Passion, spontaneity, warmth, humour, selectivity, impulsiveness, connection, communication, sharing
		"Am I loved?" or *"How is this connecting with others?"*
Earth	Late Summer	Understanding, being understood, bringing together, support, nourishment, processing/thinking, empathy
		"Do I understand?" and *"Am I understood?"*
Metal	Autumn	Efficiency, clarity, simplicity, detachment, objectivity, isolation, controlling waste, systems, precision, value
		"What's missing?" or *"What isn't done yet?"*

From reading the descriptions above, you may already have a sense of your primary *Energy Type(s)*. (Typically, we each have one or two that are most dominant.)

If you'd like to confirm your guess, you're very welcome to do *The Vitality Test*, which is a free online profiling system created by my great friend and business partner Nicholas Haines. Nick has spent his entire adult life studying, decoding and applying ancient Chinese philosophy to modern relationships and cultures to meet today's challenges.

We co-founded the *Five Institute* to further this work, and over 6,000 people around the world have completed *The Vitality Test* over the past ten years. We are frequently told that it's the most insightful personality test people have ever experienced. If you're interested, you'll find a link to *The Vitality Test* in my bio details at the end of this article.

Creating Conversations That Flow

Hopefully, you'll now have the beginnings of a happier understanding of yourself via your unique mix of the *Five Energies*. You'll find this alone eases your conversations and opens them up to greater possibilities.

We also find that people are often curious about the energy mix of people they know, including their partners, colleagues, family and friends. Some of them may be interested in *The Vitality Test* at some point. But what if they're not?

Well, here are three additional tips to smooth your path either way:

1. Stay confidently curious

If you hold your conversations with increased curiosity, you'll likely get indications of each person's energy type. And you're certainly going to find out even more about what really matters to them.

2. Actively seek to include kindness

When you are truly looking after the interests of others (not being a doormat, but generously being an advocate for good), more often than not, they'll respond in kind.

3. Aim for a transformation instead of settling for a transaction

Even a small transformation is possible, if only in how you acknowledge someone else. These three questions work wonders to *raise the gaze* and maximise those possibilities:

- What are our highest and best intentions for this conversation?
- What really matters most for us?
- How can we make this better right here and now?

By applying the ideas in this article, you'll find that your conversations will incur less friction, resistance, stuckness and stagnation.

As a result, you'll have more *Conversations That Flow*. Enjoy!

About Matthew Newnham

Matthew Newnham is a communications specialist who helps people to have workplace *Conversations That Flow*, with themselves, and with others. This enables them to get renewed clarity and confidence in their career, their business positioning, offer and marketing, and their organisational culture.

He has been a lifelong student of how we communicate with each other, starting with his days as an air cadet and officer, then as a corporate change management consultant and since 2011, as a brand positioning and communications specialist.

Along with his great friend Nick Haines, he is co-founder at *Five Institute*, home of *The Vitality Test*, completed by over 6,000 people around the world and regarded by many as the most insightful personality test they've ever experienced.

In his leisure time, Matthew is a keen club-level runner and Scottish Masters medalist competing in the 800m, 1500m and mile (and for his sins, cross country!).

https://www.fiveinstitute.com/

https://repositionme.com/

https://www.linkedin.com/in/matthewnewnham/

https://conversationsthatflow.com/

Best-Practice

Performance, productivity, efficacy, effectiveness, efficiency, fast-tracking, current best thinking, compliance, governance, due diligence

How to Grow a Leader

Lucy Barkas

"When you grow a lettuce, if it does not grow well,
you don't blame the lettuce. You look at the reasons
it is not doing well." - Thich Nhat Hanh

Leadership is not a job, - it is a way of being. Leadership is a mindset and a belief system, an outlook and approach to life. Leadership is not assigned and delivered through rank or position because there is a fundamental different between being the leader and leadership. The world is in crisis because there are too few leaders that are practicing leadership.

Leadership is not a new trend or 21st century philosophy: it is the very basis of our life journey and always has been. As we are called upon to lead our own lives, we in turn inspire others to lead theirs.

The Myth of the Natural Born Leader

You may meet some people who are *natural born leaders*. Leading appears innate, instinctive and natural, yet there is no genetic coding for leadership. Natural born leaders simply mastered leadership in their early formative lives, being nurtured and grown in an environment where their values, beliefs and strengths were supported. Leadership is so ingrained into their psyche and sense of who they are that they know no other way to be, it's as natural as breathing and thinking.

93

Yet leaders were not born this way, nor were they trained - they were grown. Their parents and carers created an environment where they developed into the leaders of their own lives, and so it follows that those leaders will in turn create environments to grow more leaders. The leadership ripple effect begins.

Leadership Crisis

The Leadership Talent shortage is real. It was first identified over a decade ago and a wave of leadership development consultants seized the opportunity to develop leaders. There are over 47 million pieces of content available online to help you understand the skills and strengths of a *leader* vs. a *manager*, so with all that knowledge you would think we would have a handle on leadership development. Yet in that decade we have seen very little traction and so the need to develop leaders is becoming critical and we need to do it differently.

Doing it differently means developing and growing, rather than training and teaching. It means creating the right environment to grow talents and brilliance. It means you stepping into conscious leadership to develop unconscious *natural born* leaders of the future.

Where parenting and formal education has failed to develop a generation of leaders then it falls to organisations to grow their talent capability and there is no time to waste. The time is now.

The following guidance is equally applicable if you are a parent of one or responsible for a global organisation. The principles for growing leaders remain the same.

Nurture Risk and Failure

In the good old days our children played in the streets, came home when the sun set, climbed trees, and led idyllic Enid Blyton childhoods, or at least that's how we like to remember it. The truth may not be so picture perfect, but our parks were full of children playing, taking risks, falling and then picking themselves back up again. As they played without parental supervision they learned their own limitations and strengths. Parents set the boundaries and then set their children free, and when they fail, they forgive and show love and compassion.

Growing leaders means that you need to create an environment where it is safe to take risks and learn through failure, after all isn't that the only real way we learn life's valuable lessons. Your job is to set challenges and goals that allow your people to stretch and grow, learn and experiment, without fear of blame, shame or retribution. You set your people free with parameters wide enough to play but narrow enough to manage risk. It is your duty to keep yourself in check and let others fail safely, learn, apply and then celebrate their successes.

Quit Being the Hero

We know you have probably solved this problem before. We know you know how to fix it. We know you could probably do it quicker yourself and that's why you are in a senior position after all. Your credentials are not in doubt, so just quit being the hero.

It feels good to rescue, fix or come up with the right answer doesn't it? That's just the rush of dopamine rewarding you for your brilliance, but this is only feeding your ego. When you are developing leaders, your ego is the last thing you need to invite into the environment. When your people come to you with a problem or need to talk through an approach, help them to find the solutions and simply ask, "What ideas have you got?"

They learn to find solutions before they come to see you and so before you jump in to give your wisdom, hold back and try curiosity.

- Ask questions to understand their logic.
- Get curious about approaches they have mulled over.
- Ask them what they think they should do.

- Listen to understand rather than listening to respond.
- Try brainstorming solutions, staying open rather than seeking closure.
- Respond positively to ideas saying "Yes and" rather than "No but".
- Nurture best thinking in others.

You may be surprised at just how capable your people are, and how quickly they build confidence in their own creativity and problem-solving capability.

Inclusion

How can you expect others to understand the consequences of their actions or buy into new ideas if they are not included in the process? If you really want to grow leaders that can operate tactically and strategically then they need to be involved in the big picture discussions. You don't need to explain every aspect of the business to everyone and often some information is business sensitive, but you do need to give your people enough rationale to understand the context and to begin making informed decisions. If your people can't make informed decisions, then question what information you are holding back to prevent their best work.

Treat people small and they will remain small. Give people room to grow and they will expand.

A Spoonful of Honesty

The self-esteem and wellbeing industry has helped organisations to understand the impact that stress, pressure, criticism and blame can have on an individuals' performance. Most people now understand that positive reinforcement and praise engages and supports peoples' engagement and motivation but too much of a good thing can be a bad thing.

A thank you sure does go along way but meaningless praise becomes, well, meaningless and the fear if criticism is leading to the holding back of critical feedback. As parents we want to build self-esteem in our children, but you also need to help them become resilient so be honest with your children about their strengths, weaknesses and approach. A spoonful of honesty is empowering and enables personal growth in responsibility.

Praise without critical feedback will not create self-aware, objective leaders who embrace continual growth and development and take personal responsibility for their actions. Your role in growing leaders is to give praise when it is due and appropriate but to also give actionable real-time feedback that enables others do learn and grow.

Without the balance either way you will not grow future leaders.

Be Vulnerable

Leader vulnerability is the ability to access real, authentic power that creates followership and is the opposite to autocratic, power over, control and command style leader-ship where people follow through fear. Unfortunately, few of us have seen the power of vulnerability-based leadership in action so it still feels a bit scary, but it is the most powerful form of leadership.

When leaders are transparent and at ease sharing their own weaknesses, mistakes, passions and purpose then people trust them. It doesn't mean they will be adored but it does mean that they are respected.

Transparency stops others wasting time and energy trying to second guess you or figure out how you want them to be or act. When you can say, "I got it wrong" or "I don't know the answer!", it empowers others to do the same. Transparency means being courageous, and don't we all want a leader with courage?

No-more cover ups, blame, second guessing or pretending. To create a business based on openness, honesty and accountability you need to lead it.

Trust

The last but most important foundation to grow leaders is trust. When your people trust you and each other, beautiful things happen. I bet you have been in a meeting where you can feel the tense under current. People are shuffling their papers or scrolling through their phones to break the tension and the fear is in the air and it is tangible. As the meeting gets underway you experience passive aggressive behaviours such as people giving others wry smiles or rolling eyes when someone speaks. You may see a colleague come under fire for some reason or another and sink into the chair or you may catch yourself shutting others down or interrupting them, so you can be heard. It is being played out in meeting rooms right now and is so normal we don't even question it.

Nobody is doing their best thinking or best work in that environment because they are in defend and protect mode – they are surviving.

Now imagine the opposite. You walk in the room and everyone is relaxed but eager. There is an expectation that everyone is on the same team and ready to solve the big issues. Each member of the team leans in to offer ideas, solutions and willingly puts their hand up to help or take a lead. The leader speaks last and acts as a facilitator rather than a director for they know that where there is trust there is no fear. You can witness people literally grow in front of you as they test their assumptions, solve big problems, ask for help and seek guidance and it feels good.

Just as a parent bursts with pride when their child takes their first step, masters riding a bike or stands on stage and overcomes their fear of public speaking, leaders feel that same joy as their people step into their brilliance. You wouldn't hold your children back, so why would you hold your people back?

True, authentic, honest, transparent and conscious leadership - grounded in trust, is how you grow leaders. Now it is down to you to choose to be part of the leadership gap solution or be part of the problem.

About Lucy Barkas

Lucy Barkas is a Leadership and Team Development Consultant who specialises in working with Leaders of 100-250 employees who want to achieve high performance through their people and culture.

With over 20 years experience with market leading businesses around the world, Lucy successfully helps leaders to understand the biggest blocks and barriers to success and together, execute a strategy to transform their businesses.

Lucy founded *Whatwhenwhyhow Ltd - 3WH* for short - to start a positive leadership ripple effect that impacts their people work, lives, communities and ultimately the world.

www.3wh.uk.com

https://www.facebook.com/LucyJBarkas

https://www.linkedin.com/in/lucybarkas

Is It Nurture Or Nature? It Is Both.

Diana Barnett

Nature Nurtures

How often have you heard someone make remarks like: "I had to go for a walk in the woods to clear my head", "working in the garden is so calming", "when I go to the mountains I am re-energised", or "I feel so relaxed and less stressed after my holiday by the beach"?

In each statement, nature is nurturing.

In this chapter, we'll explore the latest research on the relationship between nature and physical and mental health and performance and look at some specific ways leaders can incorporate the benefits and value of nature for greater wellbeing, creativity, productivity and profit.

Although we intuitively get it, progress has led to the creation of environments that make access to nature very difficult for many. However, science[1] is now validating our intuition: our gut instinct that a dose of green or blue space, even in small amounts, is good for us.

In economic terms, we pay more for locations with mountain, river and beach views. We love waterfalls, snowscapes, trees, flowers, sunsets and some of us even love to greet the sun. Our awe of nature is the reason why these are the images we prolifically share on social media.

We feel the restorative powers of nature. It goes beyond the visuals: it's also what we hear, smell, touch and taste –

a combination of all five senses. The colours, the twittering of birds, the rustle of leaves, the scent of pine, roses or lemon-scented eucalyptus, the texture of bark, leaves, grass and rocks, and sometimes the taste of teas, berries or salt from the sea. All these experiences impact on our moods and self-esteem[2].

There is a plethora of research[3] and data analysing just how beneficial nature is for us, and the benefits of connecting with it on a regular basis. Small amounts of exposure – as little as one hour a week – to either tame or wild natural environments, makes us healthier, happier and less stressed. And the more time spent in nature, the greater the results.

It appears that approximately 85%[4] of us derive direct benefit from green space and blue space.

And yet as industrialisation and technology have entrenched themselves in our lives, the time we spend in nature has declined. This adversely affects our health and wellbeing. Extrapolating the findings that we are happier, healthier and less stressed after spending time in nature, why are we not making the connection and leveraging the perks our world has to offer?

What is getting in the way?

We are dealing with an epidemic of ailments and diseases linked with our lifestyle choices, including food, environment, work, recreation, sleep, relaxation, and technology.

At home and work, ever-increasing layers of technology bring advantages our grandparents and even our parents would not have imagined. But technology comes with inbuilt stickiness[5] to keep us connected to our devices and reduce other vital connections humans need with nature, and with people through eye contact and touch.

Today's built environment is generally not conducive to encouraging us to connect with nature, thanks to the way our cities have developed over the past few hundred years with less and less green space. And yet, in the 18th century, the importance of London's parks and squares to the wellbeing of the city's inhabitants was recognised. During this time William Pitt coined the term *The Lungs of London*[6] and since then other cities around the world have adopted *The Lungs of ...* to battle for green space.

In the 19th century Melbourne, Australia drew on this philosophy and was planned and developed around multiple parks and gardens, giving its citizens and visitors access to water and green space. We believe this contributes to the health and wellbeing of the inhabitants and indirectly impacts on the liveability score it achieves every year.

It's unfortunate that many developers and authorities in the late 20th and early 21st centuries ignored the importance of green space to both physical and mental health. They also didn't understand the long term economic advantages of incorporating green space with their plans.

Thankfully the trend is changing, and the importance of green space is now acknowledged, encouraged and, in many places, mandated in development. Many new and retrofit building sites are using Biophilic design to enhance the space for visitors, workers and residents [*Biophilia* - there is an instinctive bond between human beings and other living systems][7].

A current example of retrofitting a development is *The Docklands* in Melbourne; originally built as a concrete jungle, efforts are now being made to *green* the precinct by incorporating green walls and roofs, and green spaces to make the zones more desirable for all stakeholders.

What does this have to do with leadership and work?

Research has found evidence that spending time in nature may protect against a startling range of diseases, including depression, diabetes, obesity, ADHD, cardiovascular disease, and cancer.[8] Other data has found that it can change moods and self-esteem.[9]

Our lifestyle choices affect our happiness, health and wellbeing, which in turn affects the way we operate at work. If we feel stressed, we can't perform to our best capabilities: creativity, productivity and team dynamics will not be optimal.

As leaders, we need to facilitate ourselves first, and at the same time focus on creating the space for our team members to blossom.

What levers can you pull?

Some lifestyle choices are beyond our influence, but others we can influence and encourage our team members to reap the benefit of interacting with nature.

Here are ten steps to create more connections with nature

1. Buy real plants

If your office lacks greenery, buy some real plants and position them where people congregate and meet, where their gazes fall when working at their desk. Do the same at home.

The tip here is to make them luscious, hardy, low maintenance and safe.

2. Get outside

Research shows[10] that as little as one hour a week of *intentional* walking in nature whether it be a tamed space (gardens and parks) or wild (forests and woodlands) is beneficial. During this time, switch off your technology.

Be present. Tune out and tune in, be aware of your senses responding to the environment. Use your eyes to soak up the colours and shapes, your ears to hear the birds, creatures and wind, your nose to breathe in the smells, your skin to touch the texture and physically connect.

The fifth sense – taste – is not always easy or safe to stimulate during this restorative practice, but where it is safe and non-destructive to the environment, taste what's on offer.

If you can extend your interaction to 15-30 minutes per day the benefits will be even more significant.

3. Walk and talk meetings

Where possible organise walking meetings, preferably in green spaces, where you can connect with nature and benefit from the exercise. An additional benefit is that the meetings tend not to over-run. Encourage your team members to have one or two walking meetings a week.

4. Take the meeting outdoors

Going to a meeting, to work, to the cinemas or a function? If there are parks and gardens, or strips of nature nearby, park a little further away or leave public transport earlier and take a stroll through the green space.

5. Make green exercise a habit

Challenge yourself and your team to spend 10 minutes walking/engaging in nature for 30 days, without being connected to technology. Find a way to *gamify* the challenge and encourage them to post photos with a comment on a private or open social platform.

6. Entrench the *green* exercise habit.

Research has found that it takes 30 days to shift behaviour and 100 days to entrench a habit. Create a four x 30-day challenge for you and your team. [11]

7. Recall and recount the benefits

Dedicate a few minutes in your team meetings for your team to recall and recount the impact of interacting with nature.

8. Organise important strategic events outdoors

Organise extended meetings such as strategic planning and training and development in a space that provides a connection to nature. You can coordinate some of the sessions outside and inside thus enhancing the mood, attention, creativity and productivity of at least 80% of your audience.

9. Schedule three days outside

At least once a year take time out to spend a minimum of three days in a setting that gives you maximum contact with nature with minimal contact with technology. For some, this may be wild camping while for others it will be in a luxurious accommodation without compromising on comforts. You'll benefit whichever is your preferred option.

10. Share your insights and the benefits with others

Share with me any other strategies and tactics you and your team implement to use nature to nurture yourselves.

Twitter *@Cultiv8Biz*, Instagram or email: *nature@cultivate.biz*

Hard data from around the world supports our gut feelings that nature is good for us on many levels: our health, our happiness, and our wellbeing.

Progressive leaders can embrace this movement by adopting one or more of these philosophies into practice: green exercise, green-mind, Shinrin Yoku (Forest Bathing), Biophilia and Biophilic design, or eco-therapy ...

... Nature really does nurture.

References

1. Barton. J. & Pretty J. (2010) *What is the Best Dose of Nature and Green Exercise for Improving Mental Health?* Environmental Science & Technology 2010 44 (10), 3947-3955, DOI: 10.1021/es903183r

2. Barton. J. & Pretty J. (2010) *What is the Best Dose of Nature and Green Exercise for Improving Mental Health?* Environmental Science & Technology 2010 44 (10), 3947-3955, DOI: 10.1021/es903183r

3. Williams. F. (2017) *The Nature Fix*, W.W. Norton & Company

4. Williams. F. (2017) *The Nature Fix*, W.W. Norton & Company

5. Kerr. F. Dr. (Feb 28, 2018). *Purpose.do Conference*, Sydney, Wildwon

6. *What are the Lungs of London?* - William Pitt (1708-1778) the Earl of Chatham – UK, www.historyhouse.co.uk

7. *Biophilia*, https://en.wikipedia.org/wiki/Biophilia

8. Ming. K. (Sep 16, 2015) *Immune system may be the pathway between nature and good health.* University of Illinois College of Agricultural, Consumer and Environmental Sciences. ScienceDaily

9. Reynolds. G. (July 22, 2015), *How Walking in Nature Changes the Brain*, New York Times

10. Williams. F. (2017) *The Nature Fix*, W.W. Norton & Company

11. Pretty. J. & Rogerson M. (2017) *Green Mind Theory: How Brain-Body-Behaviour links into Natural and Social Environments for Healthy Habits.* Int. J. Environmental Research and Public Health 2017, 14(7), 706; DOI:103390/ijerph14070706

• comment: (Vol 1 July2017) *Planning ahead: the mental health value of natural environments*, www.thelancet/planetary-health

• Nichols. W.J. (2015), *Blue Mind*, Back Bay Books

• Ward Thompson. C (2017) *Greenspace, health and quality of life as part of the 'Hard facts about soft values'.* Youtube.

About Diana Barnett

Diana Barnett. Born in PNG, lives in Australia. Loves travelling and would love to do more. Discovering regenerative over sustainable. Advocates the power of Masterminds drawing on the wisdom of the group, and peer-to-peer mentoring and accountability. She is motivated and inspired by Leaders who give a damn! It's about current and future generations, and our planet. Championing profitable purpose-driven businesses that make a positive impact.

Nature nurtures us; it is time to nurture nature!

Diana is a Facilitator. Curator. Podcaster. Enabler. And much more.

Find out more...

www.cultivate.biz

nature@cultivate.biz

Twitter @Cultiv8Biz

Instagram @cultiv8biz

Short Term Gain vs Long Term Profit

Simon Hammond

I run a firm of insurance brokers in the United Kingdom and we specialise in business insurance. We have been trading for 16 years now and have seen many changes in the insurance industry and economic conditions in that time. One major change in the insurance industry was the implementation in 2005 of compulsory regulation by the *Financial Services Authority*, now the *Financial Conduct Authority (FCA)*. Do I hear a collective sigh as I mention the word *regulation*?

It is commonly acknowledged that the United Kingdom is the most commercially regulated country in the world.

Regulation polarises opinion. Is regulation popular with those organisations who are regulated? Probably not. How should regulation be viewed? I'll leave that to you to answer as there will be a thousand different opinions and I am not the person to judge who is right and who is wrong.

I have strong opinions on what constitutes good customer service and how company profits should be maximised. The two are obviously linked and when you throw in regulation for good measure it makes for an interesting mix! Therefore, it was an interesting process integrating regulation into our systems, procedures and customer service whilst keeping an eye on the bottom line.

Let me tell you the story about how we won our largest client (to date) and then I will demonstrate exactly how just one part of regulation encapsulates the positive impact that good customer service can have on long terms profits at the expense of short term gain.

Like many new business start-ups, I spent the first few years of trading cold calling companies simply asking if we could provide quotations on their current business insurance. As you can imagine, I got regular responses of *"No,"* the occasional *"Yes"* or *"You've missed the renewal date, call me next year"* (which I considered to be a deferred "yes"). I always approached cold calling with gusto, refusing to be down hearted and reminding myself that I basically had a 50/50 chance of a *"Yes!"*

Just to slightly digress here for a moment, I do get asked how we win big ticket business and I'll give you a couple of quick examples.

Key Person Insurance - What if you don't?

One thing that never ceases to amaze me when I chat about insurance with business owners, Managing Directors etc. is that many do not have *Key Person* insurance. The question I always ask at this stage is, *"What would happen to your business if you, or the manager most crucial to your business, get knocked over by a bus tomorrow?"*

This is where a simple *Key Person* insurance policy not only helps the business by paying a sum of money which can support cash flow, costs of recruiting etc. but also gets that business owner thinking more deeply about the continuation of their business in the event of a catastrophe. This is where a good quality insurance broker can add value to a business.

Another example of how we win new clients is where I explain to the business owner, director etc. how one type of insurance can help companies win more business.

Professional Indemnity Insurance (PI)

There are certain professions where *Professional Indemnity (PI)* insurance is compulsory to remain accredited by their own regulatory body but, for the majority of professions, *PI* is not compulsory but can be a very effective product.

For information, if it is alleged you have been in breach of your professional duty, *Professional Indemnity* provides cover for the costs and expenses of defending that claim as well as any compensation paid to the claimant. It provides cover for *Errors & Omissions*, incorrect advice, design and specification.

But how does that help companies win more business? Well, please consider this.

If you want to tender for significant contracts for the provision of your professional services, a lot of larger companies insist on *PI* as a prerequisite. Even if it is not a prerequisite, *evidence* of *PI* insurance provided at tender stage lends weight to your offering almost as if it is a professional qualification.

PI underlines your credibility and professionalism. It says, "We're a high quality professional company, we take our obligations seriously and you have the security of knowing that if we screw up, we're insured."

Anyway, back to the story.

One company gave me a *"You've missed the renewal date, call me next year"* and, during this conversation, I jotted down all the relevant comments the Managing Director made so I could refer to my notes next year when calling again. One notable comment was that he *feared change* meaning *changing insurance providers*

The company had been with the same insurance broker for 30 years! The following year I spoke with him again and reminded him of his comments He laughed, I took that for a buying signal and gently pressed for a meeting. Fortunately, he directed me to their new Finance Director. We had a great conversation and I was invited in.

During the meeting it became quickly apparent to me that the client was paying far too much for their business insurance.

My immediate opinion was that they were over paying by tens of thousands of pounds. However, as I did not want to over promise and under deliver, I kept this opinion to myself and simply stated that I thought there would be good margins for savings.

We carried out a full market review and it quickly became apparent that the client was massively overpaying for their insurance programme.

Now, this is where some of my colleagues in the industry would sniff an opportunity of *carrying more premium* meaning they would select an insurer to work with and then ask them to increase their initial quoted premium. The insurer would charge more thus earning more money, the insurance broker would earn more commission and the client, whilst enjoying slightly reduced costs, would still end up paying more than the market rate.

Short term profit.

When I presented our findings to the client, I gave them copies of the actual insurance company quotations rather than providing our own summary. They therefore had evidence of the actual market response.

I recommended the lowest quotation we had. Cover was on a *like-for-like* basis and the premium was half of what they had been paying! I explained that we could have carried more premium but that we wanted to build a long term relationship and the only way we were going to do that was by being completely transparent from the beginning and build trust.

The client was delighted. They ended their 30-year relationship with their insurance broker and appointed us. That was over ten years ago.

In that time, the client has grown significantly and taken out various other insurances with us. We also look after personal insurance for some of their staff and I have attended various charity events they have invited me to. We have a strong relationship built on trust.

Long term gain.

Treating Customers Fairly (TCF)

At the beginning of this chapter, I mentioned regulation, customer service and maximisation of profits.

A significant theme that runs through the *FCA's* regulation is *Treating Customers Fairly (TCF)*. Indeed, there are six measurable *TCF* outcomes which is the actual evidence used by firms like us. The measurable outcomes must reflect current procedures, be kept under review and be relevant to the markets in which we operate.

I'm going to focus on the *first* measurable outcome:

Fair treatment of customers is central to our corporate culture.

Let's just think about that measurable outcome for a moment and how regulation, when integrated intelligently, can increase long term profits.

"Fair treatment of customers is central to our corporate culture." To me, that is a beautiful thing.

It perfectly encapsulates what every business should aspire to. I'm sure you already follow this principle in your own company. But is it written down? Is it in your staff handbook and employment contracts? Does it form part of your training programme? Is it in your procedures manual?

Every employee, every system and procedure, should follow this simple tenet. It should run through the core of any business. It's what turns a good business into a great business.

But how does *TCF* increase long term profits?

Remember the story of how we won our largest client, how long they have been with us now and how we now look after far more insurance for them than we did in the first year?

We could have easily carried more premium ten years ago for short term gain. But let's think about what could have happened if we did.

The client's costs would have slightly reduced.

The insurance broker would therefore have added little value. Another insurance broker could have been invited in the following year and produce the same cost savings as I did. The relationship would not be based on transparency and trust which means that the building blocks would not be in place for a long term relationship.

In short, fair treatment of customers from the outset builds long term relationships and therefore long term profits.

I bet you never thought the word *beautiful* could be used to describe regulation!

About Simon Hammond

Simon Hammond is Managing Director of *Morpheus Insurance Solutions Ltd*, Managing Director of *Morpheus Finance Solutions Ltd* and Chair of the Board of *The Executives Association of Great Britain Ltd*.

If you want to know what the other five measurable outcomes of TCF are, please contact

simon@morpheusinsurance.co.uk

www.morpheusinsurance.co.uk

www.morpheusfinance.co.uk

www.eagb.co.uk

linkedin.com/in/simon-hammond-75941949

@MorpheusInsure

Ten Strategic Questions For Business Leaders To Test the Assumptions in Your Business

Andrew Priestley

If you are like a growing number of people globally, you have probably thought about leaving your job and starting your own business.

According to the *UK House of Commons Report on Business Statistics 2017*, the number of new business start-ups has steadily increased since the global financial crisis (2009). This statistic is not limited to the UK but is in fact, part of a global trend of professionals who were made redundant, could not find employment and so decided to start their own enterprise.

Like most governments, the UK measures enterprise activity in terms of *business births* (starts-ups) and *business deaths* (ceased trading) measured over an 18 month period.

If you start your own business in the UK you have to register for *self employment* and this is most likely true for other countries.

Between January 2015 and October 2016 there were 608,111 business births; and 424,866 business deaths where presumably businesses failed to submit a self assessment. (It doesn't tell us if the business ceased trading; they simply may not have earned enough taxable income requiring them to submit an assessment. It does suggest a business death however if that business fails to submit a tax assessment in subsequent years.)

In any case, that is about 76% failure rate, which is quite significant. More so if it is your business. Your livelihood. And your money.

We know that there are about 5.7 million businesses in the UK (2017) and 75% of businesses (about 4.275M) trade below £300,000. Of that number, 80% (3.42M) have trading revenues below the *Value Added Tax (VAT)* threshold of £85,000. *(See table of current conversion rate for USD$ below).*

Dent Global's UK *12-month Threshold* accelerator programme is designed to get revenues beyond the VAT £85,000 threshold; and a 12-month *Key Person of Influence* programme specifically designed help businesses trading above £300K to create brand awareness that typcially results in a dramatic uplift in revenues.

In my case I coach and mentor business leaders to navigate through the revenues, profit and growth stages. An example is helping clients achieve five or six figure per month revenues.

The average number of staff - below £300K - is 2.4. And the average wage is £27.6K. Ideally, average *revenues per person* (RPP) employed need to average around £55K-£90K for your business to carry those wages and remain viable.

Around 1.4 million businesses (about 20%) trade between £300,000 and £2M - described as the SME sweet spot where your business delivers a profitable and reasonable lifestyle income.

At this level your business will employ between 3-20 staff, with the average about 12 staff. In any case, your recommended target *RRP* needs to be around £100K per person.

As an example a small business with revenues of £600K and six staff is a good business. However, a business with £600K and 12 staff - £50K RRP - will be struggling to make a profit; and fund growth.

About 4% trade between £2M and £10M revenues.

This is typically a business a *growth phase*, where the demands on cash intensify. This can be a testing time for your business because you are often *too big to be small, and too small to be big.*

Not surprising, a lot of businesses choose to remain trading at sub-£2M where business life is more comfortable, more predictable and profitable enough o provide a nice lifestyle income.

Less than 1% of UK companies trade between £10-50M; and a small number of companies - about 7000 - trade above £50M. And these ratios are similar in other countries i.e., USA, South Africa, Australia.

We also know that there are predictable phases in the business journey where you are specifically focused on *revenues, profits, growth, investment, scale* or maybe *exit valuation.*

If you are *not* in these performance phases then you are in the phases of *struggle, stagnation, decline, stalling* or headed for an *insolvent exit.* A reality is that too many businesses under-perform; and far too many established businesses are not saleable and the owners will exit insolvent - *owing money. In most case, both are needless and avoidable.*

What does this mean to you?

I've found that as a business leader it helps to know these broad parameters, to better understand where you currently sit within the business landscape. And where you want to or need to go.

For most businesses, if you are trading below £85,000 and wanting to grow, choose incremental revenue targets such as £120K, then £250K then £300K. If your goal is to be a high performing business experiencing faster growth, there is a greater need for clarity on the strategic objectives and how you intend to achieve those outcomes.

In my experience, people have a good idea for a business, but the business lacks a clear strategic direction. As they say, *without a vision the people perish.*

For example, its useful to know that you only become profitable when you have a predictable, stable, recurring revenue base. Most sub-£300k businesses are stuck in the constant cycle of *chasing revenues.* High growth indicates you have learned how to lock in stable recurring revenues, to be profitable enough to fund the growth phase.

We know that the average small business start-up will borrow £25,000; and the average corporate escapee (a professional who leaves corporate life to start an enterprise) will invest on average, £75,000 - usually their redundancy payout.

When I do business trainings and workshops I notice many attendees struggle to answer basic strategic questions and often answer from the context of where they are current-ly. When I explain business statistics and concepts like stages of stage of revenues and RPP they start to see the strategic direction more clearly.

For example the company that employs 12 people has to either increase revenues or shed staff. Currently they are trying to be all things to everyone - another strategic mistake - and have a sales-averse culture. They can all do the work but no one whats to chase that work!

If a client wants £1M in revenues and they are currently at £100K they need a dramatic uplift in revenues. Naturally the discussion is how they envisage achieving that result. If they lack the cash to fund that growth they can seek investment, of course, but often an incremental or organic uplift is more likely.

Outside of your revenues, and regardless of whether you are a start-up or an established business, I've found the following strategic questions are thought provoking in assisting leaders to scenario plan your next move.

And I have found the same strategic questions are invaluable as a discussion starter for your team or the basis for a periodic performance review.

I have found it best to discuss rather than write your responses and I highly recommend actually recording the discussion on a Voice App; and then having your answers transcribed into a report.

As a guide, allow yourself 90 minutes to answer all these questions in one sitting to get an overview. Then go back and focus on each question individually in more detail later. One client took ten days answering one question a day over two weeks.

Start with your current best thinking. And, by the way, if you don't know an answer say, "I don't know." That is useful because it highlights the gaps in your strategic thinking.

The ten strategic questions

Here are ten strategic categories of question to reflect on. They seem basic but take your time and talk them through thoroughly:

1. **Your Purpose and Vision** - Why did we start the business? Why does our business exist? Exactly?

2. **Your Core Concept/Idea** - What is the core business idea? What do we do? (Try and be concise.)

3. **Your Preferred Customers** - Who exactly is the *target customer* for this business, what problems do they have that we solve and what is the core proposition for those customers?

4. **Your Team** - Who is on our *internal* operating team (staff)? Who do we need on our team? Who is on our *external* team (suppliers)? Why them? What are our resource gaps?

5. **Your Marketing/Sales** - What is our route to market? What is the sales journey for a customer? And, who are our competitors and what is *their* route to market?

6. **Your Products/Services/Price Points** - What products and services do we sell; and for how much? Why those items? What do we need? What don't we need? What do our competitors sell?

7. **Your Numbers** - Do the numbers stack up? How do we know the business is working? What do we measure and why? How does your accountant measure out success?

8. **Your Business Model** - What is our business model? Are we retail, wholesale, e-commerce, online, etc? Are we a boutique business or scalable? How do our products and services get from us to our customers? What infrastructure needs to be in place and controlled to ensure our business model works?

9. **Your Systems** - What systems and processes are needed to grow and scale? (NB: the difference between businesses that thrive and perform are documented systems.)

10. **Your Insights** - OK, what did you learn? What are our key insights from this exercise? What's working? What isn't? What are the gaps? Where are going - exactly - as a business? What needs to happen in the next 90 days?

Cross reference your responses

I hope you notice that several of the aspects link naturally to other aspects of the business; for example the business idea ... and what you sell. Going to market ... and sales performance. Business model ... and your team.

Once you have answered these questions, cross-reference your answers and look for obvious and subtle connections.

As a business coach I often find my clients gain powerful strategic insights about their business, simply by getting them to explore their current best thinking to each of these questions *and then look for obvious cross links.*

Answering these questions and cross referencing you responses usually delivers invaluable business insights.

Check the assumptions

Importantly, in reviewing your answers ask these three time-tested strategic questions:

- What is our *current* best thinking?
- What are you *assuming* to be true? and,
- What would need to *prove to be true* in order for this business to work?

These are powerful questions because I find clients' answers often have an embedded assumption that infers a best case scenario. For example, if you have decided your target client is a high net worth individual then you are assuming that high net worth clients exist, and that you have an accessible route to that market.

An accounting firm recently decided that their target client has at least £25M in property and assets. Their plan was to create an accounting division specialising in finance and tax advice. *That market exists*, but they underestimated the requirements to access this market.

It has been a long and slow process but after several years they are finally gaining traction in this space. Hanging in there was only possible because their accounting services was under-writing this activity in the start-up phase. Had this been their only revenue stream they probably would not have survived the first 12 months.

This activity is especially useful if you are writing or reviewing your business plan. It does not replace business plan writing but it will provide meaningful strategic input; and will make a difference to your top and bottom line.

Starting!

I hope you try the 90-minute activity. If you would like the questions to be fleshed out with more detail, theory, case studies and anecdotes then please check out my best selling book, *Starting!* on Amazon.

Starting! is available in both Kindle and paperback.

Will you lend me £25,000?

The above questions came about from working with seasoned VCs and angel investors. If you ever watch *Dragons Den (BBC)* or *Sharks Tank* you will notice the business gurus ask similar questions - or variations on the above categories- to decide if they will invest in the business, or not. Essentially they are executive summary type questions covered in any business planning process.

But let's now test if you learned anything from this article.

Let's pretend I come to you and ask, "Will you lend me £25,000 for my business?" What questions would you ask me? I think you will find your questions will be very similar to the one's listed above.

If so, you are thinking more like an investor.

I hope that you are beginning to understand that *you* are the primary investor in your business. As a business leader you have a responsibility to not only identify if you have a *good idea* for a business, but that you have ...

... a *good business* for your idea.

References

- *http://researchbriefings.parliament.uk/ResearchBriefing/ Summary/SN06152#fullreport*

- Dent Global - https://www.dent.global/

Currency Conversion (GBP£/USD$/AUD$) (April 2018)

GBP£	USD$	AUD$
85K	120.2K	156.6K
300K	424.4K	552.8K
1M	1.4M	1.8M
2M	2.8M	3.6M

About Andrew Priestley

Andrew Priestley is an award winning business coach, speaker and bestselling author. of three business books.

Qualified in psychology he was listed in the top *UK 100 Entrepreneur Mentors*, 2017.

He coaches and mentors business leaders worldwide.

www.andrewpriestley.com

https://www.linkedin.com/in/andrew-priestley-tce/

https://www.facebook.com/groups/leadershipgigs/

@ARPriestley

Emerging Trends

**Innovation, disruption, new thinking,
gaps in the market, emerging industries,
emerging trends, transitions, transformations**

Business Intelligence Leadership

Robyn Wilson

What is *Business Intelligence Leadership* you might well ask? *Business Intelligence Leadership* is something that I like to refer to as 360-degree leadership. It is the full scope of the leadership spectrum that encompasses not only one's ability to have an extensive grasp on subject matter, but also the character of great leaders, intuitive problem solving based on knowledge, experience and advanced linguistic skills.

A *Business Intelligent Leader* or a *BIL* displays all the qualities of a great *Human Leader*, think Martin Luther King or Sir Winston Churchill. More specifically a collective of *Intelligence (IQ), Emotional Intelligence (EQ), Cultural Intelligence (CQ)* and *Advanced Linguistics (AL)*.

This article will review the qualities of a *BIL* for you as a leader in this Millennium (and as a leader of Millennials). I will answer the question "What is it that you need in your leadership toolkit that will not only fully equip you to survive but to thrive in the post information age amid the *Artificial Intelligence (AI)* revolution?"

Leaders, as you may well already know, are distinct from *Managers*. Unfortunately, there are many who have not made this distinction and tend to manage rather than lead.

When coaching and mentoring CEO and *Small to Medium Enterprise (SME)* business owners one identified that he was having issues around conflict management in staff resulting in reduced performance and sales. He wanted to lead his staff but was *stuck* in managing. He therefore appointed a manager to take over the day to day running of the manufacturing business supposedly allowing him to step back from managing and up to lead. The difficulty was he still wanted to maintain *control* and felt he was not able to delegate full responsibility to his manager.

Further into the coaching sessions it was revealed that he had undertaken very limited professional development in his lengthy career which exclusively revolved around manufacturing processes and practices. It was certainly not directed on developing the self personally or professionally into the leader he wanted to be.

I am sure you already know, the best investment you can make in yourself is in your personal and professional development. This is also where the value of *EQ* becomes critical.

Two people of equivalent of similar *IQ* but very different *EQ* placed into positions of leadership the one with the highly developed *EQ* will most certainly be the better prepared leader and most often the one selected for promotion.

EQ is such a critical aspect of success in leading firstly self, then others in teams and ultimately community. If one is unable to lead self successfully then it is obvious that there will be complications when leading others.

Nature and nurture has a lot to answer for and it is imperative to dissolve any negative or unwarranted emotional respons-es from the past that are impacting the present, along with any limiting beliefs or decisions, internal conflict or ongoing anxiety. This process of unlearning and then relearning is achieved with the assistance of *neuroplasticity* of the brain and its ability to make new neural connections resulting in positive behavioural change.

How do you do this you may ask? Firstly, recognising that you have barriers that are impacting on your success and then finding a leadership coach and mentor who is trained in neuroplasticity and neuroscience techniques to resolve issues that are at the Unconscious level (out of awareness).

To determine what my limitations were when I hit my *glass ceiling* in a national corporate role I participated in a 360-degree *Multi Factor Leadership Questionnaire (MLQ)* where I obtained feedback from peers, those I supervised and my leaders.

This identified specific areas on which to focus my leadership development with the assistance of a leadership development plan including accountability from a neuro-leadership mentor and coach. This process took me on the pathway that I wanted to go very fast. It involved not only new learning but a great deal of dissolving or unlearning conditioned responses from the past that were setting up a flight or fight instinctual response in times of extreme pressure.

From bitter experience, I knew this was no longer serving me and I resolved to take many steps to dissolve, unlearn and relearn. That is the beauty of the brain. *You can teach an old dog new tricks.*

A further complication in today's ever-changing world are the effects of technology or more specifically the rise of AI replacing the professional knowledge worker. This has caused some angst amongst those climbing the corporate ladder in search of lofty leadership heights.

How can you as a leader future proof yourself and keep ahead of the challenges that facing you in this AI society and what makes a *BIL* stand out? What puts this leader ahead of the pack able to lead new generations of not only people but AI? To answer these questions a *BIL:*

Will lead not manage
The *BIL* must know and exhibit the qualities of a leader as opposed to those of a manager. They must have vision, see the

big picture and remove themselves from the day to day running of the business, corporation or organisation. They are smart enough to know that they can hire highly skilled others to *do* or *manage* while they lead.

Display the characters of leadership

Some people say leaders are *born and not raised*. I tend to believe that *leaders can be born and raised*. People can change their behaviour and develop character. Leadership skills can be taught but according to Sarros et al executives who lose their jobs are frequently dismissed because of behaviours of poor character. William Hendrix discusses in the foreword for Sarros et al times of action decision making in the cut and thrust of the life of a corporate leader the personal ethics and behaviour that is informed at a deeper level by their values will determine the good character of the leader or not.

Has great intuition

Great leaders have learnt through experience and research to be able to *trust their gut* and to be able to think on their feet so that in times of extreme pressure when *life or death* decisions need to be made they can go with their primal instincts.

How do you develop the ability to do this is a good question? It is a combination of experience from the past and learning from your mistakes, reflection when you are given feedback, and having a wealth of knowledge on many topics that you have to draw upon (a great leader is constantly reading and learning).

It is also being mindful and practicing mindful leadership - getting in touch with your body and it's reactions to emotions or the triggers (red flags) that are a *tip off* to situations that require thought before action or action without thought.

Is empathetic

By not buying into the spin, rhetoric, the story or the argument this leader is savvy enough to be able to listen and remain emotionally detached. Not in a cold way but in a way that *acknowledges* rather than *understands* therefore being *empathetic*, rather than *sympathetic*. This leader knows that each person has their own *model of the world* and sees, hears, thinks and feels differently about any one given set of circumstances at any one time, even if they are sharing the same space and time with another person.

This is where their *Cultural Intelligence (CQ)* is so important particularly as business is carried out across the globe with other leaders in real time.

Empathetic leaders will not *judge* but they may need to *adjudicate*. Whether you are male of female empathy is a required characteristic of a great leader. If you are not able to *put yourself in another's shoes* even just so you can *try on the problem* or the *perceptual position* of another then I advise that you add this into your personal and professional development plan for the coming year.

Is a great communicator

The saying *two ears and one mouth* is one that the *BIL* lives by. They know that they will learn more by listening and asking relevant questions from their team or trusted advisors to be able to make informed decisions.

They are able to read sensory acuity (the fine reactions in the face or behaviour of others), eye patterns to determine areas of access of the brain, hears and sees sensory predicates in verbal and written language to know what the other is feeling. They are an advanced linguist and know how to reframe and be flexible in their language to get the result that they want and is the best in any situation.

Is always learning

Knowing that everyone you meet is a source of knowledge and perhaps has a perspective that you have not is something that the *BIL* thrives on. They are constantly reading, watching, soaking up like a sponge sources of information, commenting on and reading the comments of others to open their minds and souls to the wealth of free-flowing information that is out there for everyone to tap into.

The exciting thing about the *BIL* is that they can take a wide variety to sources of information and value add every time. They are visionary and see the future, the big picture and know where they want to steer their ship and that of others who will follow them and come along for the ride.

I am loving working with *Business Intelligent Leaders* assisting in guiding them to reach their full potential and watching them smash their glass ceilings. It would be a pleasure to hear how you smash yours in the future.

References

- James C. Sarros, Brian K. Cooper, Anne M. Hartigan, Carolyn .J Barker. (2006) *The Character of Leadership – What works for Australian leaders- making it work for you.* John Wiley & Sons Australia Ltd

About Robyn Wilson

Robyn's career has spanned 34 years in the education and training fields. Robyn focuses on working with established SMEs to develop what she calls *Business Intelligence Leadership*.

Through her own leadership development, she discovered the theory and practice of Neuro-Linguistic Programing, Time Line(r) Therapy and Hypnotherapy.

These modalities have helped Robyn to transform not only her own life but many others. It has led her to reach her desired success including the dream and goal of writing and publishing a book in 2018.

Using neuroplasticity or the brain's ability to unlearn and relearn to create new pathways in the neurology of the brain leading to new behaviours and success, Robyn works in a collaborative approach to assist others to break through their barriers to success and excellence.

Web: robynwilson.com.au

LinkedIn: https://www.linkedin.com/in/robynwilsontrainingcompany/

Email: robyn@robynwilson.com.au

Why Leapfrogging Innovation in Governments Requires More Than Technology

Michele Scataglini

This article is a call for action for government leaders on how to unlock value for citizens and society. It explains the importance of technological innovation in driving government transformation, its complexity and how technology fits into the broader picture of value creation, that is grounded in purpose and delivered via innovation strategy.

Solving societal problems and contributing to the welfare of people is the mandate of governments and their leaders.

Recent megatrends in technology disruption, budgetary constraints, citizens' growing expectations for transparency, accountability and quality in public services, create an additional complexity that require rapid and radical rethinking of governments strategies.

While technology provides an opportunity for value creation, the issue of government transformation is a more complex and sensitive one, as it affects the lives of billions of people and involves huge financial resources. The digital transformation of governments could free up to $1 trillion annually in economic value (McKinsey & Company, 2014), which could be purposefully redistributed towards the socio-economic development of citizens and communities.

The diverse approaches of three leading strategy and consulting companies, exemplifies complexity.

The first one (McKinsey & Company, 2016), highlights the operational aspects of utilization of digital technologies in public service delivery.

The second (KPMG, 2014), captures the importance of using digital technology in the policy development, monitoring and evaluation cycle.

And according to the third (EY, *2015*), transformation starts with the identification of a clear purpose, reflected in the transformation of operations through an agile approach covering technology, human resources and organizational structures.

A common threat identified are cyber-attacks. Conversely, the approaches treat to a lesser extent the societal costs that a digital government transformations may imply, such as redundancies created by increased efficiency through the application of robotics process automation in back-office functions, or the marginalization of stakeholder groups excluded from services due to the lack of skills or infrastructure.

Based on this review, digital transformation of governments is a complex matter and seizing the opportunities and addressing the challenges it implies, requires a thorough strategic approach that considers both policy and operational aspects and is guided by purpose.

The role of government leadership now is most important than ever: it requires a purposeful intent, going beyond a political and short-term mandate and skills for strategic management of innovation.

While purpose is ingrained in humanity, the conscious leader should enable purpose activation across organizations.

According to recent studies (EY, *2015*), organizations that have a clearly identified purpose, have more loyal customers, employees and create greater shareholder value. The same applies to governments, clients-citizens, employees-civil servants and the economic value created.

The government purpose should be identified, agreed and owned at the highest level of the organizations and then activated at the lower operational ones. Human behavioural experts and learning tools (workshops, web-based learning, books) can be used to enable the process, but there should be full ownership at the highest levels.

Once the purpose is clearly identified, the second point for the leaders is how to define an innovation strategy that can help to deliver that purpose. It is necessary to stress attention on the difference between innovation and digital transformation, as the latter is an element of the first.

For the sake of exemplification, let's assume that the purpose of a certain agency is to *enable citizens to age healthily and actively*, then the question for leadership is to define the right mix of technology, build the rights systems and organizational models that allow to create this value.

The methodological framework on *Innovation Strategy* of the Saïd Business School, University of Oxford (*Ventresca*, 2017) provides thought leadership and guidance on this matter. Technology is a key aspect as it generates opportunities for value creation (M. Ventresca, 2017). Several experiments in this sense have already taken place in Governments.

In Iceland for instance, in the context of the 2008-2011 Constitutional process, the drafting of sections of the constitution was crowdsourced online (LSE, 2014).

In the Enfield council of London, a robot called Amelia helps citizens to locate information and complete standard applications as well as simplify some of the council's internal processes (The Guardian, 2016).

Similarly, in Lithuania, Robbie Insomnia is a new employee in Lithuania's National Paying Agency of the Ministry of

Agriculture, analysing reimbursement requests on European Funds (National Paying Agency, 2017). Blockchain applications are also being piloted, by humanitarian organizations to deliver financial aid to refugees in Syria. In relation to public policies, the United Nations promote the use of Big data to evaluate the results of public interventions.

Technological inventions per se however are not sufficient to deliver citizens' value. Government leaders should have the capability to design an ecosystem of stakeholders around that technology, made of providers, users, partner government agencies, that can contribute to creating value and appropriate of a part of it (Normann & Ramirez, 1993).

Managing this ecosystem is a complex task, which can generate economies of scale, of innovation, lower the cost of service delivery and ensure the widest coverage of the population. To exemplify things, we can think of government like the *Amazon* marketplace where the citizens buyers can access services that are produced by *Amazon* (e.g. *Kindle*) or third parties (e.g. sellers, logistic partners).

While respecting data privacy of citizens, governments could reap additional benefits by further adopting open data policies (Chesbrough, 2006), i.e. making available (big) data to private parties, for solving societal problems through the development of new services.

Again, drawing analogy from the private sector, the multinational Procter & Gamble has grown exponentially by implementing an open platform for product development (Proctor & Gamble, 2016), meaning that hundreds of its products have been ideated by non-employees.

It is easy to understand that experimenting innovative technologies and recombining them with the capabilities of different stakeholders is a different task from those depicted in traditional job descriptions, and which requires different evaluation metrics and possibly different organizational units.

In other words, the process of driving innovation in governments and public service delivery could be considered like an internal start-up.

Once again, drawing from examples of the private sector, there is evidence that successful organizations (O'Reilly & Tushman, 2016) are those that create organizational capabilities to explore new opportunities for value creation while exploiting existing ones. In other words, the government leaders should ensure continuity and improvement in service delivery using existing capabilities, while exploring radically new ways of doing so. Not only this requires separate organizational structures and different skillset for talent, but also a process for rapid, efficient and effective prototyping and testing of novel approaches.

A massive cultural change in government organizations is necessary if these objectives are to be achieved. Leaders need to create an open communication towards civil servants, especially in organizations that are territorially spread.

Employees should feel empowered to take decision within the leadership defined path, and short-term wins and failures should be celebrated collectively.

We do not expect governments to change overnight into *GoogleX's* moon-shots factory (RE:WORK, 2016), where managers receive bonuses or promotions to interrupt a project in its early stage, before massive losses are made, but it will be sufficient to remove a culture of disempowerment that sometimes affects the public sector.

To conclude, government leaders today more than ever, have a terrific opportunity to create a massive change in the quality of life of people and future generations. This requires firstly a conscious choice, going beyond personal gains and short term political mandate. Second, it requires strategic skills to develop government innovation strategies by blending the right technologies, ecosystems and developing organizational capabilities to create policies and citizen services.

Last there is a need for a cultural shift at all levels of the government organizations, that is united around purpose, empowered by trust, and embracing both achievements add failures as moments of celebration.

References

- UN Global Pulse, 2016. *Integrating Big Data into the Monitoring and Evaluation of Development Programmes*

- O'Reilly. C. & Tushman, M., 2016. *Lead and Disrupt: How to Solve the Innovator's Dilemma*

- Chesbrough, H. W., 2006. *Open Innovation: The New Imperative for Creating and Profiting from Technology*

- Coindesk, 2017. United Nations Sends Aid to 10,000 Syrian Refugees Using Ethereum Blockchain

- EY, 2015. Purpose-Led Transformation

- KPMG, 2014. *Reprogramming Government for the Digital Era*

- LSE, 2014. *Iceland's 'crowd-sourced' constitution*

- McKinsey & Company, 2014. *Public-sector digitization: The trillion-dollar challenge*

- McKinsey & Company, 2016. *Digital by default: A guide to transforming government*

- National Paying Agency, 2017. *New employee at National Paying Agency – robot!*

- Normann, R. & Ramírez, R., 1993. *Designing Interactive Strategy.* Harvard Business Review

- Procter & Gamble, 2016. *Connect + Develop*

- RE:WORK, 2016. *"Culture Engineer" Astro Teller on failure and brilliance*

- The Guardian, 2016. *Robot Amelia – a glimpse of the future for local government*

- Ventresca, M., 2017. *Technology, Market and Organization Framework for Innovation Strategies.* Saïd Business School

About Michele Scataglini

Michele Scataglini is a focused and resilient professional, passionate about contributing to the improvement of the quality of life of people and future generations. He advises private corporations and governments to design and implement innovation strategies for value creation.

Michele has 17 years of professional experience and 10 at EY. He has successfully delivered over 40 projects in 15 countries including such clients as the *European Commission, World Bank,* and many national and regional governments in the EU and third countries.

Michele has studied *Strategy and Innovation* at Saïd Business School, University of Oxford and holds a BA (Hon's) in International Economics, from Trieste University, Italy.

www.michelescataglini.com

https://www.linkedin.com/in/michele-scataglini/

https://twitter.com/MicheleScatta

Did you miss Fit-For-Purpose Leadership books #1 and #2?

Relax! Both our best-selling Fit-For-Purpose #1 and #2 are available on *Amazon* as both paperback and *Kindle*. A collection of inspired leaders worldwide give their highest-value, current best thinking on business leadership.

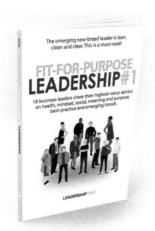

Join Leadership Gigs

Would you like to be a part of *Leadership Gigs*? *Leadership Gigs* is a conversation for leaders worldwide. Here's how it works.

Think of it like a private members club – you can dip in and dip out as you wish – there is no pressure to show up.

Currently it is free to join. A good way to start to get involved is by requesting to join our *Facebook* group:

http://bit.ly/LeadershipGigsFB

Leadership Gigs is a support network so if you need high-end help/support then ask the group (you'll be nicely surprised). Our aim for this is to build a thriving community of leaders who are helping each other's journey into the next decade.

Lastly, thank you for purchasing *Fit-For-Purpose Leadership #3.* I would love your feedback.

Watch out for *Fit-For-Purpose Leadership #4*, coming soon!